From
Difficult
to
Delightful
in
Just 30 Days

How to Improve
the Behavior of
Your Spirited Child

JACOB AZERRAD, Ph.D.

McGraw·Hill

New York   Chicago   San Francisco   Lisbon   London   Madrid   Mexico City
Milan   New Delhi   San Juan   Seoul   Singapore   Sydney   Toronto

The McGraw·Hill Companies

Library of Congress Cataloging-in-Publication Data

Azerrad, Jacob, 1936–
    From difficult to delightful in just 30 days : how to improve the behavior of your
spirited child / Jacob Azerrad.
        p.   cm.
    Includes index.
    ISBN 0-07-147039-5 (alk. paper)
        1. Problem children—Behavior modification.   2. Discipline of children.
    I. Title.

HQ773.A97   2006
649′ .64—dc22   2005035669

1 2 3 4 5 6 7 8 9 0   FGR/FGR   0 9 8 7 6

ISBN 0-07-147039-5

McGraw-Hill books are available at special quantity discounts to use as premiums and
sales promotions, or for use in corporate training programs. For more information, please
write to the Director of Special Sales, Professional Publishing, McGraw-Hill, Two Penn
Plaza, New York, NY 10121-2298. Or contact your local bookstore.

The information contained in this book is intended to provide helpful and informative
material on the subject addressed. It is not intended to serve as a replacement for
professional medical advice. Any use of the information in this book is at the reader's
discretion. The author and publisher disclaim any and all liability arising directly and
indirectly from the use or application of any information contained in this book.

The case histories presented in this book are real. However, names and other details have
been changed to protect privacy.

This book is printed on acid-free paper.

From Difficult to Delightful in Just 30 Days

To Suzanne, Jeffrey, Colin, and Lauren,
my children and grandchildren,
with love

CONTENTS

❦ ○ — ○ ❦

FOREWORD

SHORTLY AFTER THE discipline of psychology declared its independence from philosophy several hundred years ago, most of its professionals hitched their wagon to the coattails of psychiatry in an effort to better understand normal and pathological behavior. The "medical model" reigned supreme throughout the ensuing centuries. Reading the early history of this adventure, one encounters the excursions into laborious assessment strategies, along with the familiar terminology and mysterious concepts that defined much of psychiatry. Prominent among the thinking of this age is the attribution of unconscious and preconscious mechanisms to account for undesired (if not pathological) functioning, along with the genetically endowed controlling mechanisms such as traits and instincts for which there is little optimism to expect satisfactory treatment or cure.

Especially when professionals are asked to intervene on behalf of a child's actions and behaviors, the standard fare has been to espouse the party line that there is a need to understand. There is always the hope that eventually there will arise the good fortune to "outgrow" behavior problems or that the child will luck into the cutting edge miracle drug that will finally save him or her. Technical and popular writings by experts of many colors have been advocating this message in books, articles, and appearances in the media.

Things did not get much better for many decades, at least until the miraculous advances of pharmacological medications seemed to offer an avenue of hope; no longer was the accepted explanation for inappropriate behavior to be seen as the result of inner forces and perhaps prenatal influences but rather as a biology gone wrong. This exaggerated conclusion was rather quickly shattered in the face of mounting criticism against the growing pill culture and the fostering of a drug dependence to address psychosocial functioning. Evidence of frank prescription abuse together with the failure to live up to the expected promises to cure what needed to be cured persuaded both physicians and patients to look elsewhere for help.

To be sure, many generations of clinical psychologists, psychiatrists, and other "mental health professionals" continue to champion the psychodynamic methodologies in which they were trained but perhaps with greater skepticism than their elders and mentors. Only in the relatively recent past has an acceptable alternative been proposed and a different set of treatment technologies been developed, viz. a behavioral and learning based approach.

Such an approach gained scientific respectability from the countless basic science animal studies and human experiments that culminated in a behavioral therapeutic model. Increasingly, such programs were discovered by the many suffering clients and their caregivers as rational, efficient, and welcome solution alternatives.

The hungry public that seeks solutions and remediation for the concerns they seek became a strong force in continuing the rejection of flawed therapies and mythological theories and has made impressive inroads in educating the wider audiences of health-service providers and consumers alike. One need only reflect on the striking success of television productions such as "Nanny 911"; once a learning-based environment is introduced in the seemingly complex and intertwined world of home, proper behavior can be dramatically restored in a matter of days. When parents are able to face up to their responsibilities by learning some basic parenting skills that foster learning of proper behaviors, and when the child is able to master some easily acquired repertoires, the former horror scene involving sibling, adult, and child interactions are then played out with civility and mutual respect in a seemingly magical setting.

Jacob Azerrad was trained as a traditional clinical psychologist. Over the years in his extensive practice, he became disenchanted with the dynamic approaches he had been using and discovered the behavioral approaches that he continues to use to this day. He is not only a master clinician, but he has also become an advocate for more rational and effective therapeutic strategies. With a sharp pen and a gift of wit, he has produced a most readable work that is chock-full of serious, practical, and valuable ideas for restructuring failed behavior patterns.

Such a book could only come from a therapist who has had extensive exposure to a variety of behavior problems and who has been able to achieve huge successes in dealing with his clients. It is must reading for anyone who owns a child!

∞

DAVID MOSTOFSKY, PH.D.

Professor of Psychology

Boston University

PREFACE

⟨◦———◦⟩

IF YOU'RE THE PARENT of a difficult child and you follow the simple, commonsense steps described in this book, you will see a remarkable turnaround. In less than a month, tears will give way to smiles, tantrums will be replaced by cooperation, and "no" will turn to "yes." I've seen it happen a thousand times.

The success of this program doesn't depend on any form of medication. In fact, the reckless, unwarranted use of prescription drugs can be a huge part of the problem.

It doesn't involve blame—not for the parent, nor for the child. Blame is a just a way of explaining why something fails. This approach doesn't fail.

And it's so simple, you can do it yourself. You don't need a doctor or therapist. You don't need to have a degree in psychology or to wade through a thousand pages of mumbo jumbo.

Best of all, you don't have to wait until your child is ready for Social Security before you see the results. The results start right away.

But you've got to follow the steps. None of this happens until you make the changes described in this book. When you do, you will dramatically improve your child's life. And, of course, your own as well.

That's a promise . . . mine to make, and yours to keep.

Acknowledgments

THERE ARE A great many individuals without whom this book would never have become a reality. The most important of these individuals is Henry Scammell. Henry has taken what I have written and transformed my words and sentences into an extremely helpful book for parents whose kids are driving them crazy and who are on the verge of giving their children medication for what in the past were considered ordinary childhood misbehaviors.

I would also like to thank my mother. She fortunately did not read the parenting books currently in print. These books all too often teach parents to protect children from the ordinary slings and arrows that are part of everyday life. Strong-willed children are believed to need a protective or "user-friendly" environment or, in reality, an "emotional bubble." As a result, we have generations of children who have never learned to handle the ordinary disappointments of living. This book, in large part, is the product of my resilience and ability to handle disappointment and my never having experienced a "user-friendly" environment.

I would also like to thank John Aherne, my editor at McGraw-Hill, and my literary agent, Peter Rubie. They have both been extremely supportive and helpful toward the goal of making this book a reality.

Many thanks to Susan Buckley, who has worked tirelessly on the many changes, deletions, and updates that resulted in the final manuscript. Having worked with me for well over a decade, she has responded to my many imperfections with humor and grace. Joan Curtice has also been extremely supportive and most helpful in terms of both her creative and organizational skills. She has been an invaluable source of encouragement and support long before the first words were put on paper.

Last but surely not least, I feel fortunate to have two wonderful children. To Suzanne and Jeffrey, who make it all worthwhile.

People in power have a vested interest to oppose critical thinking.

—Carl Sagan

❦ ◦———◦ ❧

The tenacity with which these theories were kept alive in the analytic community . . . despite the fact that their therapeutic application did not improve the patient's condition, reflects the strength of an ideological structure disregarding clinical facts.

—American Psychiatric Association, 1989

PART ONE

HOW BEHAVIOR HAPPENS

1

WHAT DO
CHILDREN WANT?

DON'T BE PUT OFF by the chapter title's paraphrase of Sigmund Freud's famous rhetorical question about women; you won't find much else that sounds like Freud in this book. The reason for that absence lies in the answer to the question. Children don't want psychiatrists or psychologists, and they don't need them. They don't need drugs. What they want and need is parents.

Why? Because all behaviors are learned. Sainthood is not a drug-induced behavior, and neither, in most cases, is brattiness. Saints learn to be saintly. Monsters learn to be monstrous. Childhood behaviors, in which all such life paths begin, cannot be prescribed by psychiatrists; they are learned, first and foremost, from the mother and father.

But parenting is learned as well, and for the last four generations many of America's parents have been taught the wrong skills. Under the misguidance of a library-full of parenting books based on Freudian concepts, parents have taken on the role of therapist, nurturing the very behaviors that are driving them crazy. They have been encouraging children to be unhappy, fearful, needy, and difficult in their relationships with others—and the way they have been taught to do it is by rewarding just about everything their children do that is inappropriate, destructive, or self-defeating.

Now, with government intervention, the problem has taken an ominous new turn. In the past few years, the number of children on behavior-modifying drugs has skyrocketed into the tens of millions. These are not the so-called recreational contraband from faraway shores, but mainstream, mind-altering pharmaceuticals manufactured in America, prescribed by physicians, and administered by parents and school nurses across the land.

Childhood behaviors, in which all such life paths begin, cannot be prescribed by psychiatrists; they are learned, first and foremost, from the mother and father.

What's happening to the children of America? How did we come to accept this wholesale, mindless marketing of folly, not just of drugs but also of basic, causal concepts of behavior and responsibility? Who taught the parents these costly mistakes that have become so ingrained in our culture? Why are they so counterproductive? Can they be unlearned? Is the damage reversible?

This book starts with the behavior issues that so often lead to such negative outcomes for the children—and for parents and for our culture as a whole. It offers a proven, commonsense response to the challenges and opportunities of parenting, focused on the natural, systematic nurturing of the qualities of character and maturity that author Daniel Goleman has labeled as emotional intelligence.

2

FOUR GENERATIONS OF BAD ADVICE

❦⟶❦

FOR ALMOST A CENTURY, self-proclaimed experts in child rearing have been leading the public down a primrose path. They have persuaded millions of followers, especially well-educated, well-intended, middle-class mothers and fathers, that their children's misbehavior is a symptom of a psychological disorder. The only way to deal with these disorders, they argue, is for the parents to start thinking of themselves—and relating to their children—as therapists dealing with patients. That mind-set, in a nutshell (a carefully chosen metaphor), has become the problem.

How many of those same parents today would accept the proposition that once we become adults, none of us is really responsible for what we do, regardless of how immoral or criminal? How many would agree that humans are no different from other animals, with no soul or spirit? Who still believes that everything issuing from our brains is nothing more than the result of chemistry? Or that the root cause of neurosis is simply morality and that we can't be truly healthy until we break free of its suffocating strictures? Today very few thinkers—I would hope none at all—still buy into this type of nihilistic nonsense. But at one time, these beliefs comprised the catechism of behavioral theory, and in one degree or another each of them still lingers at the core of the shaky science to which millions of parents have unquestioningly entrusted the education and socialization of their children.

The Medical Model

It all began with Sigmund Freud. Because Freud was a physician, it is not surprising that he developed a medical model to explain the human psyche. A medical model of psychological processes views aberrant, disruptive, or dysfunctional behavior as a disease; examples of that behavior are referred to as symptoms, and the name of the specific behavior or set of behaviors is called a diagnosis. And because Freud's vision of those psychological processes was not explainable in the limited vocabulary of physical disorders, he invented a whole lexicon of words and phrases—including id, ego, superego, complexes, and the oral, anal, and phallic stages of human development—to meet that need.

Let's take a look at how the medical model describes a simple, commonplace childhood problem. I did my internship in the department of psychiatry at Children's Hospital Medical Center, in Boston. One of the psychiatrists there, a woman who had been educated in the Freudian tradition, was treating a boy of 10 on an outpatient basis for enuresis. She explained the situation in a fairly straightforward manner; beyond giving it a Latin name, there aren't too many ways to dress up the simple facts of bed-wetting. Her treatment of the probable cause of this condition, however, was a far different matter. She told us that the little boy's problem was the result of one of two possible disorders. In the first diagnosis, he was fixated at the anal level of psychosexual development and was peeing in his bed because he was repressing feelings of anger at Mommy, creating more work for her with the daily supply of soiled and smelly bedsheets.

If you like that one, you'll love the second choice. Although only 10, her hapless patient had entered the phallic level, a slightly more grown-up stage of development, and the bed-wetting was a disguised expression of something else. I'll never forget her words: "Symbolically, he is putting out the fires of repressed sexuality toward his mother." This may make perfect sense if you're the kind of adult whose courting rituals include peeing on the furniture, but for the behaviorists in her audience, both explanations were greeted with smirks—disguised, repressed, but smirks nonetheless. For a behaviorist, the reason for the little boy's problem was simply that he was a heavy sleeper, and he still hadn't learned to break out of that heavy sleep in response to bladder tension.

The way physicians acquire their skills is the same way as the rest of the world: by learning. They learn to read, they learn to write, and they learn arithmetic. There is little argument that good manners are learned as well. So, why does it stop there? Why aren't bad manners, thoughtlessness, and rude and selfish behaviors such as lying, throwing, and greediness all learned equally with other mechanisms for coping with life, and as subject to being relearned in more appropriate ways? The answer is that the medical model is based on disease and pathology, not on wellness and common sense. As an explanation of human behavior, the medical model has always been a forced fit—illogical, counterintuitive, and historically a hard sell. As noted, Freud responded to the challenge with a new vocabulary, but that was just the start. The battle would rage for generations.

The Totalitarian Vision

The strategy was militant and aggressive, and the tactics were often subversive. In 1927, for example, a psychologist named Ralph Truitt set an ambitious goal for the Division of Child Guidance Clinics of Great Britain's prestigious National Committee on Mental Hygiene: "If we are going to prevent dependency, delinquency, insanity, and general inadequacy," (all good things to be against, even by today's more relaxed standards) "the schools should be the focus of our attack." A few years later, with Britain's entry into World War Two, the attack metaphor proved equally compelling to John Rawlings Rees, who had previously served his country as deputy director of the "clinic" responsible for Britain's psychological warfare program. He proclaimed: "We have made a useful attack upon a number of professions. The two easiest of them naturally are the teaching profession and the Church; the two most difficult are law and medicine. . . . If we are to infiltrate the professional and social activities of other people, I think we must imitate the Totalitarians and organize some kind of fifth column activity! If better ideas on mental health are to progress and spread we, as the salesmen, must lose our identity. . . . Let us all, therefore, very secretly be the fifth columnists."

The term "fifth column" is worth a closer look. It was coined just four years earlier, during the Spanish civil war in 1936, when the Nationalist general Emilio Mola was besieging Madrid with four columns of troops. Asked by the press whether he thought that was enough men for the job, Mola responded that he had a fifth column within the city, secretly (and treasonably) working on his behalf. *The Oxford Dictionary of Phrase, Saying and Quotation* defines *fifth column* as "an organized body sympathizing with and working for the enemy within a country at war or otherwise under attack." The phrase was widely used in that meaning in England, where the war with Germany raised fears of subversion by Hitler's numerous British sympathizers. Fifth columnists were—and are—traitors. Especially in view of Britain's circumstances at the time, it seems astonishing that Rees would use that particular metaphor. But it was not simply a poor choice of words or a semantic mistake: it was entirely consistent with his advocacy of attack, infiltration, and deceit.

It is obvious that the strategy was historically successful, though perhaps less in terms of Truitt's stated targets—dependency, delinquency, and so forth—than in the length of the occupation. The eventual outcome was to split the educational system's focus between learning and mental health, essentially securing the beachhead for the successful fifth columnists. Teachers may still stoke the furnaces on the modern ship of learning, but for at least the last half century in America, the helm has been solidly in the hands of psychologists. Rees's totalitarian vision is now a reality.

Teachers may still stoke the furnaces on the modern ship of learning, but for at least the last half century in America, the helm has been solidly in the hands of psychologists.

The Mumbo Jumbo Factory

The victory didn't come without a built-in problem. In order to stay in charge, psychologists had to keep renewing the argument that they were really needed—which meant they could never claim complete victory over the bugaboos that gave them their power. They do that by a process described in Edward Shorter's recent *History of Psychiatry* as the systematic pathologizing of human behavior. "Take, for example, the question of boyhood," Shorter says. "Whereas once Tom Sawyer-esque enthusiasm was seen as part of the natural spirits of ladhood, in the 1960s and after, a whole series of psychological diagnoses arrived to define such behavior as pathological. The bidding opened high, with 'minimal cerebral dysfunction' as it was called. . . . Tom Sawyer, in other words, had brain damage."

That new diagnosis, clearly intended to be alarming, turned out to be so scary that it wasn't that easy to sell. In a few years, it was replaced by another term, "hyperkinetic reaction to childhood," that got more or less the same reception. Although neither term lasted for more than a few years, each reinforced the notion that something seriously wrong was going on in our children's heads. Having laid that groundwork, the mumbo jumbo factory went into high gear. The result of that third great quest to name a condition that previously didn't exist was "attention deficit hyperactivity disorder." Under this new banner, psychiatrists began writing prescriptions in record numbers. Today more children in America's schools—in excess of six million of them—are taking Ritalin for ADHD than are being treated for teenage acne.

Such is the legacy of Sigmund Freud, preserved and improved by a legion of disciples from Benjamin Spock to T. Berry Brazelton. Dr. Spock, author of the bestselling book *Baby and Child Care*, was remembered in his obituary chiefly for telling parents that "kids don't have to be disciplined into adulthood but can direct themselves into adulthood by following their own will." Apparently, he never read *Uncle Tom's Cabin*. Compare that advice to the answer of the parentless Topsy when asked who made her. This paradigm of giddy, purposeless confusion replied, with poignant insight, "I 'spect I growed."

A few years ago, I dropped in on a colleague at his vacation home on Cape Cod. His son Benjamin, then 5, was playing with a toy fire truck on the floor while his parents entertained their guests. As the adult talk became more animated, Benjamin's motor and siren sounds rose in volume as well, in obvious competition with the visitors. Finally, after the guest next to me leaned forward, cupped his ear, and asked our host to repeat his last remark, the colleague looked in his son's direction but without a word or any other signal of admonition, apparently just waiting for a break in the racket so he could continue the conversation. If the father was unwilling to act on—or even acknowledge—this implicit cue from his guest, Benjamin was not; he recognized immediately that the request was a comment on the din he was creating, and it was just the reaction he had been hoping for. He arose from the floor, lifted his metal fire truck over his head in the manner of a cherubic King Kong, and brought it down on his

> Today more children in America's schools—in excess of six million of them—are taking Ritalin for ADHD than are being treated for teenage acne.

guest's leg with enough force to open a gash from knee to ankle.

I'd like to think that what happened next could have taken place only in the home of a psychologist, but I know better. Too many of my clients have told me stories of their own about responding "by the book" to outrageous behavior by their children. In this case, the father leaned forward solicitously, his tone calm and soothing, his entire focus on his son, with no concern at all for the plight of the injured adult. "Benjamin," he said, "sweetheart." Meanwhile the guest leaned forward as well. My own reaction was astonishment, first at what had just happened and next in the mistaken impression that the victim was about to enter into this soulful communion with the little assailant. Soon enough, though, it became apparent that he was not bending down to reassure his attacker, but rather because he was in agony. Still oblivious, the father took Benjamin firmly by the arm but only to draw him into a loving, paternal embrace. "We don't do that kind of thing," he said. "We don't hit our guests with fire trucks."

Benjamin's response was to return the hug, but without much enthusiasm, and as he turned away on the break, he shot a sly look at his victim that eloquently contradicted everything his father had just said. *Of course we do that kind of thing. I just did it.*

The Collapse of Discipline

Signs are everywhere of children being led like Topsy or Benjamin into head-spinning misery—for themselves and for those around them—by their own will. The signs are in the eyes of desperate parents seeking help, in the skyrocketing sales of medications into a multibillion-dollar industry, and in the disturbing, chaotic, often violent behavior of the children themselves. This systemwide collapse of discipline parallels the rise of such atrocities as street and schoolyard stabbings and shootings. Instead of the order that children crave and which is available only through thoughtful, deliberate discipline and firm parental leadership, the slighted child is forced to settle for a diagnosis from a parent who has become the child's therapist.

Decades of research have proven that this approach is not only ineffective in treating behavior problems but also is now the main cause of such behaviors. Indeed, the more "sophisticated" parents become about the mental health issues that allegedly underlie bad conduct, and the more conscientiously they pursue their roles as unlicensed mental health professionals, the worse their children are likely to behave. I have been in practice for more than a

> This systemwide collapse of discipline parallels the rise of such atrocities as street and schoolyard stabbings and shootings.

third of that century and have witnessed the growing epidemic of troubled, self-centered, and out-of-control children.

3

THE NEW DRUG EPIDEMIC

❈⟶⟶❈

SOME THIRTY YEARS AGO, the first lady of the United States became the figurehead for a tough-sounding national program aimed at stamping out the use of drugs by children. Since then, however, the government has lost whatever credibility it might have had as an advocate for just saying no. Instead, it has become the principal supplier of behavior-modifying drugs to American children, starting with preschoolers and extending to graduation and beyond. Its impact on this country's youth is bigger than the Mafia, bigger than the Golden Triangle of the Middle East, bigger than the Colombian cartels. And under the aegis of the No Child Left Behind Act (sometimes referred to by educators and physicians as No Child Left Undrugged), it is financed by America's taxpayers and protected by its laws.

Miracle Pills

The problem began more than a generation ago with the emergence of the first psychotrophic drugs for the treatment of mental illness. By redressing imbalances in the chemistry of the brain, many of these new medicines produced nearly miraculous results in the management of illnesses that had long been considered intractable. Millions suffering the terrible mood swings of manic depression (now called bipolar disorder), for example, found they could control their symptoms and return to productive living simply by taking a daily pill.

But dramatic solutions are seldom as simple as they first appear. Today, in our market-driven economy, it takes several years and costs $880 million on average to bring a new drug to the consumer. Because the stakes are so high, competition is intense, and pharmaceutical companies are motivated at least as much by profits as by any desire to serve the common good. Whenever there is a conflict between the two, the first impulse is to protect the company's investment and secure its market share; the impulse to do good comes in a distant second to the urge to do well.

It was recently revealed that the maker of the arthritis medicine Vioxx had suppressed its own data and dismissed the claims of others that the drug increased the risk of fatal heart attack and stroke by up to fivefold. Eric Topol is one researcher who reported the drug's fatal flaw, but his warning was ignored. In an October 2, 2004, editorial in the *New York Times* headlined "Good Riddance to a Bad Drug," he wrote, "The Food and Drug Administration could have forced Merck to do the appropriate research studies, but instead it was a bystander." In mid November, one of the FDA's own drug safety reviewers told Congress the agency's culture "undervalues, disregards, and disrespects drug safety," and instead of regulating drugs, it treats the industry like a client. The reviewer concluded, "We are virtually defenseless."

Nobody could accuse the government of being a bystander in the forced drugging of our country's children. America's watchdogs not only have opened the door to the henhouse but also are working hand in glove with the fox. Today the federal government is right beside the pharmaceutical industry in pushing for the mandatory mental health screening of fifty-two million students and the six million adults who work in public schools. An essential element of that plan is mandatory medication.

Over a period of several years, that same government stood idly by as the number of teenagers who took their own lives while on antidepressants began to climb. By the fall of 2005, finally forced by public pressure to acknowledge the obvious, the FDA ordered that antidepressants must carry a "black box" warning of the risk of suicide. Where did the pressure come from? The decision was made only after it was revealed that fifteen clinical trials over several years had demonstrated such a link and that the analyses of those studies had been suppressed by many of the companies that had sponsored them. In fact, the FDA itself had suppressed the analysis by its own expert that first demonstrated a link between these antidepressants and suicides among teenagers and children. Prozac was the only such drug that the FDA had already approved for adolescent depression, but others of the same type, called selective serotonin reuptake inhibitors, are routinely prescribed for the same condition and must now carry the warning.

There is still no such black box notification required for some of those drugs' other side effects, which include several types of diabetes, stroke, convulsions, pancreatitis, cardiomyopathy, arrythmia, and interference with the menstrual cycle. But even if there were, who would read it? A first grader is certainly not going to refuse a pill because of some warning on the container—in fact, most schoolchildren on mood-altering medication never even see the bottle it comes in.

Ritalin: The Silver Bullet

The government-sponsored forced drugging of children comes nearest to Alice-in-Wonderland in the nearly incredible story of the most popular drug of all, Ritalin. As virtually everyone knows, Ritalin is the silver bullet that slays the dreadful dragon of attention deficit hyperactivity disorder, which has become a part of the national vocabulary by its initials, ADHD. Both Ritalin and ADHD have been around a long time. Thirty years ago, when the drug was new and the disease it treated had just been given a name, the number of children on Ritalin jumped almost overnight from zero to 150,000. By 1988, it reached a million. By 2000, six million children were taking Ritalin. Today that number is about to double again. If the numbers are to be believed, Ritalin is saving America from an epidemic that is growing almost as fast as the wonder drug can be manufactured.

But what, exactly, is ADHD? Astonishingly, Dr. Paul Lieber, of the FDA, says he doesn't know—and neither does the government: "As yet, no distinctive psychophysiological disorder of ADHD has been delineated. . . . I have yet to receive anything which would constitute proof of an abnormality, one that can be tested for patient by patient when proving that we are not drugging entirely normal children." A colleague, Dr. Lawrence Dillar, replies, "The reason why you have been unable to obtain any articles or studies with any clear or confirmed evidence of a physiological abnormality . . . associated with ADHD is that there is none." Lieber concludes, "The many millions of schoolchildren around the world who are being drugged have no disease."

If you remember Nancy Reagan's one-line slogan for the war on drugs, you probably also recall that some critics at the time thought "Just say no" might be a bit simplistic. But in view of today's tremendous upswing in childhood drug use, maybe it was too complicated. Tens of millions of doses of these so-called ethical drugs—in this context, an oxymoron of the worst kind—are prescribed by doctors and administered by school nurses every day.

Take Massachusetts. Between 1988 and 2003, prescriptions of stimulants, antidepressants, and antipsychotics to children rose more than 300 percent. In early 2003, the *Boston Globe* reported that one out of every nine children aged 6 to 12 who were enrolled in the state's Medicaid program was taking psychotropic medications. And if you think they got better as they got older, you'd be wrong. For teenagers, the number of users rose to one out of every eight. The problem wasn't limited to children on public assistance: that particular patient population just happened to be the easiest to measure. The state's secretary of health and human services described the pattern by which psychiatric medications were prescribed to children as "haphazard" and "quite extraordinary." In response, the president of the American Psychiatric Association—for whom a principal mandate is defense of the status quo—cautioned against overreaction.

Profits Versus Ethics

The worst pushers are the giant drug companies. Billion-dollar public relations and marketing campaigns to the contrary, their primary goal is not to create healthy children, or to increase learning and coping skills, or to improve the human condition. Instead, the companies spend hundreds of millions of dollars on the legally questionable and ethically despicable practice of advertising directly to the patient (or more precisely, to the patients' parents and teachers) in a deliberate strategy of bypassing the physicians, who will then be pressured to write the prescriptions. Many times the ads don't even tell the reader or viewer what the drug is intended to do—partly because that would involve unsupportable claims, and partly to avoid explaining the drugs' side effects.

What's going on here? Is it possible that America is really facing a gathering epidemic of depressed, psychotic kids? Or, are the defenders of the phenomenon right when they argue that the behavioral problems have been with us all along, and the explosion in prescribing patterns is due to the fact that these wonderful drugs weren't available until around the middle 1980s?

Growing up is not a condition. Childhood is not a disease.

There's an old proverb (or there should be) that warns, if you plan to buy cloth in the thieves' market, be sure to take your own yardstick. The pharmaceutical industry and American medicine have been selling parents a short bolt for decades. They've been getting away with it because they have been using a yardstick with only about three inches to the foot. Their yardstick is the medical model for the measurement of human behavior.

That model says that if a type of behavior works, it's healthy, and if it doesn't work, it's sick. Translated to parenting, if your 3-year-old is drawing inside the lines of the coloring book, you don't have a thing to worry about, but if he or she is executing that same artwork on the wallpaper, the stage is being set for a clinical diagnosis. That's where the pills come in.

There are pills for yelling, biting, throwing, kicking, cursing, punching, name-calling, and lying. There are pills for whispering in class. There are pills for when Grandma dies. There are pills for bad habits and mistakes of judgment. There are pills for daydreaming.

Short-Circuiting Learning

What's wrong with the medical model of behavior is that it deals with learned responses as though they were diseases. And by prescribing strong medicines instead of teaching children new choices, it short-circuits the process by which they grow and learn. Worse, it lays the tracks for a lifetime habit of responding to challenge and disappointment with avoidance, denial, and chemical dependency.

It's easy enough to see this same pattern when the subjects are not children, but adult alcoholics. The way a drunk responds to good news is with a drink. Ditto with bad news—or any kind of change or shock or crisis. The alcohol is a liquid insulation that buffers the drinker from the experience of living, from the chance to learn and grow, from the feelings and sensibilities that give existence meaning.

You don't have to be a Shakespeare fan to appreciate these lines from *As You Like It*:

> *Sweet are the uses of adversity,*
> *Which, like the toad, ugly and venomous,*
> *Wears yet a precious jewel in his head;*
> *And this our life, exempt from public haunt,*
> *Finds tongues in trees, books in the running brooks,*
> *Sermons in stones, and good in everything.*

That "precious jewel" is the increased awareness—of ourselves, of the power and beauty of the world around us—that comes with knowledge. And the way we get knowledge is not from pills, but from learning. Growing up is not a condition. Childhood is not a disease. The world is filled with slings and arrows; they are an essential part of how we grow. The medical model of behavior has been thrust upon us by default. It is wrong-minded and corrupt. It is stealing the jewel of life experience from America's children.

The current medical-model-based books on child rearing promote a "bubble" concept, protecting normal children from adversity in much the same way as an artificial environment of sterile plastic protects immune-deficient children from germs. By shielding perfectly healthy kids from the kinds of experience that smooth and temper personality and character, this approach deters or inhibits the development of an emotional immune system that will carry them safely into adulthood.

It's time to just say no to drugs for kids. Some states have already passed laws that prohibit manufacturers from advertising psychotropic drugs directly to the consumer. Some have made it illegal for them to talk about their products with teachers and school nurses. Nevertheless, in the great majority of states, those practices are still legal, and you can be certain the drug companies are pushing their products in those states with all their might and guile.

I t's time to just say no to drugs for kids.

Your preschool children are far too young to defend themselves. It's up to you as the parent not only to say no to drugs but also to start teaching again. Children need to be shown that life is meant to be learned and experienced, and that it's not just a pill to be swallowed and an ordeal to be avoided.

4

CHANGE YOUR
CHILD'S WORLD

THE PROBLEM IS NOT in the kids at all. In almost every case, it is in how they are being taught.

A Program That Makes Sense

In the first week of the program offered in this book, the premise of parenting is returned from misguided and discredited psychotherapy to one of case-proven common sense. This is followed by a step-by-step preview of the coming three weeks, in which the family dynamic is realigned in a healthy, natural balance.

Let's start with some case examples of "problem" children, taken from my notes at the initial interviews with their parents.

George, 3, whines or cries for attention and for fulfillment of his every need. He hits playmates and parents; throws things; bangs things when he doesn't get his way; screams when he doesn't get a requested video, doesn't want to take a shower, or doesn't want to come to dinner; and fights with his brother. Dad is reluctant to intervene with firmness, because he says he doesn't want to "break his spirit." Where did he get that nonsense? . . . From a book on child care.

Freddie, 2, is described by his parents as "stubborn as a mule" and "a mini Robin Williams." He needs 100 percent attention, doesn't want to go to bed and is up at 1:00 A.M., doesn't want to let others speak, pushes, hits, and kicks. His parents dutifully hug and comfort him, but despite the short-term benefits of this approach, the problem only gets worse.

Olivia, 4, cries for long periods when she doesn't get her way and is easily frustrated. An only child for her first two years and the first grandchild on both sides of the family, she views her 2-year-old sibling with intense rivalry. When her mother gets her a plain Band-Aid to apply to a small scrape, she shrieks until it is replaced with the requested Barney brand. Her behavior reminds her father of a temp who worked briefly in his office—constantly in need of attention, endlessly complaining, and insistent on performing new tasks in ways she found comfortable and familiar but that placed unnecessary burdens on others. It worries him that his child will grow into an adult whom people will be glad to be rid of.

Clarise, 5, cries frequently and says nothing is right: her hair isn't combed the way she wants, she won't wear the clothing put out for her, breakfast is not to her liking, she doesn't want the blue cup. She pinches, pushes, yells, and calls her parents stupid. The more they respond with all the prescribed assurances and reinforcements, the worse she gets. They're determined to keep on loving her, but some days that's harder than others. And they wonder if maybe she's right about their being stupid, at least as a judgment of their parenting.

Ethan, 3, is described by his mother as "meltdown boy." Since reaching 18 months, he has erupted at the slightest provocation, pinched, yelled at his younger brother and told him to shut up, and struck out at all the family members. His parents have read many books on the difficult child, all to no avail.

Max, 4, has been difficult since age 2. He screams a lot, interrupts his mother on the phone, jumps on her back, hits his mother and sister, throws toys, pushes kids, threatens to break other children's possessions, and needs 100 percent attention. On one occasion, when stopped from choking another child while at play, he explained, "I was trying to tell him it was my turn."

Catherine, 3, responds with tantrums when things do not go her way, when demanding ice cream after dinner, when a video is not available, when she wants to wear inappropriate clothing. She screams, throws things, slams doors, and on occasion has bitten herself. Her family "walks on eggshells."

Jamie, 4, doesn't listen, hits other children, talks and acts disruptively at family gatherings, and is described by his parents as a "bull in a china shop."

Tyler, 5, threatened and once spat on his teacher, doesn't listen, refuses to brush his teeth, refuses to go to bed on time, and uses defiance in school as a way of demonstrating that he is a big boy. "I know there are big boys—and grown men—who act that way," his mother tells me. She adds, "Part of me says he'll grow out of it. Another part is worried that he's giving us a preview of what he's going to become."

Probably some of these examples are familiar, based on a situation in your own household that led you to buy yet one more book on child care. Don't be alarmed by any similarities. Not one of these situations involved brain damage or any other form of pathology. None required drugs or expensive therapy. In fact, the defiance and hard-mindedness of difficult children are an expression of something worthy: the desire to be grown up.

Toward Personal Accountability

The problem is that children often choose the wrong way to reach that goal. Parents who ignore those wrong choices in the hope that they will correct themselves are likely to be disappointed. Defiant kids who are allowed to "win through intimidation" will often grow into adults who use the same behavior—and continue to make life miserable for everyone around them. Children who are protected from the consequences of their destructive behavior will continue that behavior—and will continue to be isolated and perplexed in their relationships with others—until they learn the hard lessons of personal accountability.

This book describes a time-proven technique for channeling that same impulse—the urge to grow up—into more productive, creative, responsible, and mature directions. Using that technique, every one of the annoying, destructive, or inappropriate behaviors described here was corrected and reversed in less than thirty days.

5

ALL BEHAVIOR IS LEARNED

❖

BESIDES THE FACT that they were both famous singers, what did
Karen Carpenter, who died of anorexia, have in common with the
pathologically overweight Mama Cass? In what way did saintly Mother
Teresa resemble out-of-control prizefighter Mike Tyson? And what trait
did alcoholic Janis Joplin share with her apparent opposite, teetotaler
and temperance firebrand Carry Nation?

The answer is that all of them *learned* the behavior that either ruined
them or made them a saint. In the negative examples, the behavior
turned into a childhood habit that wound up as an adult addiction. I
can't resist the observation that Mother Teresa turned into a habit (the
clothing of a nun) as well, but while the behavior that led her to holy
orders would define her character for the rest of her life, there are two
reasons it cannot be labeled addictive. First, the term is limited to
learned responses that are destructive to the person employing them.
Substance addiction, such as the uncontrolled use of alcohol, tobacco,
or other drugs, along with other forms of addiction such as to violence,

overeating, or systematic self-starvation, always leads to serious negative outcomes, sometimes including death. The second reason is that addiction involves the ceding of control—and therefore the abrogation of responsibility—for individual behavior. These are exactly opposite to the conditions of sainthood, in which positive behavior produces beneficial results for all concerned, and that same admirable behavior, even when habitual, is always a matter of deliberate choice.

Unbreakable Habits

Karen Carpenter learned to deal with emotional crises through the avoidance of foods. Although Mama Cass may appear to have done the exact opposite by overeating instead of starving in times of stress, on a psychological level the two responses were nearly identical. Both were learned young, beginning as childhood mistakes that remained uncorrected until they became unbreakable—and fatal—bad habits.

Substance addiction, such as the uncontrolled use of alcohol, tobacco, or other drugs, along with other forms of addiction such as to violence, overeating, or systematic self-starvation, always leads to serious negative outcomes, sometimes including death.

Mother Teresa modeled her life on the example of saints. One can assume that this choice reflected her family's value system and that she made the decision and first acted on it early in her life. It's safe to make a similar assumption about Mike Tyson, who learned to answer his childhood fears with violence and to take by force what he could not earn by skill—whether in robbing a senior citizen of her groceries in a housing project elevator when he was 12 or trying to steal an opponent's claim to the world heavyweight boxing title by biting off a portion of his ear.

Rocker Janis Joplin, an icon of the rebellious 1960s whose raucous, defiant life on the edge was fueled by drugs, alcohol, and an exuberant talent, died of a heroin overdose in 1970 at the age of 27. By contrast, housewife Carry Nation had never touched a drop and was twice that age before anyone ever heard of her. But in 1900, when she finally picked up her hatchet to chop her way into her first Kansas saloon— and into American history as the godmother of Prohibition—she too was demonstrating a pattern of learned behavior. The behavior Joplin had learned was avoidance, in her case by using substances to enhance good experiences and blunt painful ones. (Another unforgettable example of avoidance is the fictional Scarlett O'Hara, who never shed her charming, spoiled little-girl habit of dealing with adversity by not thinking about it until "tomorrow.")

Carry Nation could hardly be called an avoider; in her rage against alcohol, which had wrecked her first marriage, she came to believe that she spoke with the voice of God and that her violent extremism was sanctioned by the Bible. That behavior was not the product of idealism or even of rational thought. It was the legacy of a tortured childhood in a family riddled by mental illness, most particularly her mother's delusions. She is remembered by history as a feisty little woman; before they got the vote, all women were similarly minimized regardless of physical stature. In reality, however, despite fragile health in her early youth, by her late teens she was nearly six feet tall and physically as powerful as most men. And what she had learned by then was not the fine art of negotiation or the power of passivity. The one great lesson to emerge from the pain and chaos of that sad start was that what worked best in redressing wrong and knocking down life's obstacles was simple, unrelenting rage.

Warning Signs

That brings us back to George, Freddie, Olivia, Clarise, Ethan, Max, Catherine, Jamie, and Tyler, whose capsule biographies appear in the previous chapter. It was obvious to me from hearing their stories that each of them, in his or her particular way, had come to pretty much that same conclusion. They were learning the same kind of behavior that catapulted Carry Nation and Mike Tyson onto the national stage and that was already causing those nearest to them all kinds of grief. It is highly unlikely that any particular child, no matter how difficult, will ever approach that level of notoriety, but it would be a huge mistake to ignore the warning signs in the hope that with time they will be self-correcting.

> It would be a huge mistake to ignore the warning signs in the hope that with time they will be self-correcting.

So, how do we go about helping them to unlearn their errors and change the direction of their lives?

6

ALL PARENTS
ARE TEACHERS

❧ ⊶ ⊷ ❧

FOR BETTER OR WORSE, all parents are teachers. In most cases, loving parents have loving children, and parents whose lives lack self-control teach out-of-control behavior to their children. Based on modeling alone, however, positive or negative behavior in adults is not always certain to produce that same behavior in their offspring: not every child wants to imitate a saintly mother or heroic father, and children of alcoholics, to pick a negative example, can be so frightened by the experiences of their youth that they become teetotalers in adulthood. Still, regardless of the outcome, positive or negative behavior in adults is guaranteed to have an impact on the way the children grow.

In this new model, the parents have to learn to become teachers. Doing so begins with recognition of some basic facts of life that constitute the theme of this book. For a start, you don't teach mature, responsible behavior by rewarding its opposite. The one sure test for evaluating advice from the so-called experts is whether it encourages—with undeserved positive attention or with inappropriate permission—the very childish behavior it is intended to reverse. Further, there is a vast and fundamental difference between compliance and learning. A child can be drugged into acceptable behavior on a short-term basis, but in addition to the other ethical issues of unwarranted and coerced use of mood-altering pharmaceuticals, the dependency that their use engenders lies in the opposite direction of the goals of successful parenting.

Three Goals of Successful Parenting

So, what are those goals? Basically, children need to learn just three things.

First, they need to learn that all of us live in a world in which disappointment is a part of being human. We wish all learning were easy, but it's not. There is no "smart pill" for getting an education without a lot of hard work. The frustration we can remember from our own childhoods at deciphering the symbols of language or mathematics, for example, is a form of disappointment in that wish. The same applies to childhood hopes for the immediate and complete satisfaction of our requirements for food, attention, love, admiration, acceptance, or any of the other physical and psychic

> In most cases, loving parents have loving children, and parents whose lives lack self-control teach out-of-control behavior to their children.

necessities. In order to lead successful lives, children need to acquire the skills to handle that disappointment calmly and in a manner that doesn't get in the way of learning and growth.

Second, they must be led to understand that we

The reason a child first believes all other life revolves around his or her own is that in the first few months, it does.

all live in a world with other people whose needs, feelings, and wishes must be understood and respected. Do you remember what happened when Galileo discovered that the earth revolved around the sun, rather than vice versa? Although the solar system was several billion years old, science was still in its infancy, and the institutions of learning and authority responded with childlike intolerance. The reason a child first believes all other life revolves around his or her own is that in the first few months, it does. Empathy—the ability to understand and identify with another's situations, feelings, and motives—is an acquired skill. This doesn't mean teaching children to become victims or to always put their own interests behind everyone else's. It does mean teaching the ability to recognize and weigh the wants and needs of others along with their own. Empathy is the basis for friendship, cooperation, and the joint striving toward shared goals that distinguish a civilized society from a barbarous one. It is—or should be—the basis for marriage and parenting. We have to take the time and effort to understand the feelings of our children. If we're impatient with the process, we are certain to be unhappy with the results.

And third, children have to be taught how to control their behaviors. This isn't limited to stifling the impulse to bite a sibling or to smash a visitor with their fire engine, and it's more than not hogging all the marbles, stomping their feet, or throwing food. It means controlling everything they do to achieve their needs or in response to events. Self-control protects the family, friends, schoolmates, and others who are around your child from actions that are inappropriate, disruptive, or destructive. Of equal importance, it protects the child from the consequences to him- or herself of such behavior. But self-control is about far more than avoiding the "shalt nots" in life; by fostering a class of responses we call Mother Teresa behaviors, it equips your child for dealing positively and constructively with life's challenges.

Two Disciplines of Instruction

As a first step toward achieving these goals, the parents are instructed in two disciplines: looking at their children with new eyes; and keeping a diary of their children's behavior. While both of these are novelties for most parents, they are standard procedure for a teacher. Every new student is evaluated by the teacher when they meet for the first time at the beginning of the school year, and the student's subsequent progress is chronicled in a series of written appraisals. The most familiar forms of these appraisals are daily grades on tests, projects, and papers; periodic report cards; and parent-teacher conferences at the end of each semester. These two exercises are equally valuable teaching tools for the parent.

Your primary focus is shifting from the negatives to the positives, and what you're seeing with your new eyes is a lot more encouraging than what you saw with the old.

In the diary, the parent records specific examples of the child's meeting the three basic goals listed in the preceding section: dealing calmly with disappointment, developing empathy in the form of sibling caring and Mother Teresa behaviors, and learning self-control. These categories of new behavior are simply intended to describe any instances, such as seeking to make Mom's or Dad's life easier, in which the child's focus is on pleasing another person—the opposite of self-centeredness and one of the surest signs of growing up.

Parents are asked to look for and record six to ten examples of these behaviors weekly. They almost always tell me they see positive changes in their children simply because they are looking at them from this new perspective instead of responding primarily to the kind of behavior the children have been using to get their attention. Because they are looking at their children with new eyes, they are also praising them without being told to. It's analogous to the principle in the social sciences that it is not possible to study any individual or population without changing it. This interaction implicitly encourages the child to behave appropriately, resulting in fewer incidents of tantrums, hitting, and throwing. The anger diminishes significantly because you have found a new way to meet one of your child's most basic needs.

A Positive Shift

Something else is changing as well. Your primary focus is shifting from the negatives to the positives, and what you're seeing with your new eyes is a lot more encouraging than what you saw with the old.

Very early in the process, once you recognize your role as a teacher and are properly equipped with these two basic tools, you'll discover that it feels a whole lot better to be a parent.

7

COMMON SENSE DOESN'T NEED A DIAGNOSIS

⟨⟨∘———∘⟩⟩

Now THAT WE'RE TAKING the first few steps along the road to reason, let's pause a moment to consider what frequently happens when a parent seeks counsel from the healing art of psychotherapy, the popular alternate route in the treatment of a difficult child. Almost always, the therapist frames the problem as the consequence of either temperament issues, stages in the child's development, or conflicts raging within the child's head, and in place of reassurance or helpful advice, what the seeker winds up with is a diagnosis. No doubt, temperament and development stages are factors, but they are far more responsive to a behavioral approach than to a medical one. If the diagnosis happens to be something trendy, such as ADD or ADHD, the parent is faced with the difficult task of treating a disorder that is so elusive of definition that critics say it doesn't really exist.

A Modern Tragedy

Except for the difference in scale, this process is not that far removed from the demon hunting that went on in Salem three centuries ago. However, that scale difference is significant. The witch trials of 1692 claimed a relative handful of victims: although hundreds were accused and dozens arrested and jailed for months without trial, only nineteen were hanged on Gallows Hill, and one man of 80 was pressed to death under heavy stones—not because he was found guilty, but because he refused to stand trial. By contrast, an accusation of ADHD usually comes in the same breath as sentencing, and the number of children now being medicated with Ritalin for this phantom disorder is in the millions. And if you as the parent don't agree with the diagnosis (bring on the rocks), all that proves is that you weren't paying attention—and in many cases your child gets treated anyway.

What are the implications of this modern tragedy for its participants? For that small minority of therapists who prescribe years of counseling in search of a demon that usually doesn't exist, it can mean a guaranteed annual income. For the child in such cases, it means the same length of time with no improvement in the "condition" or in the behavior that brought the child into therapy in the first place. For the family, it means terrific expense with no return—and unnecessary added years of disappointment in which they continue to be held hostage to the child's unacceptable—and easily correctable—behavior.

> No healthy child should be kept in a bubble of chemical-based emotional isolation during the years when the child is supposed to be growing up.

In that majority of cases in which the behavior is treated medically instead of through counseling, the therapists make up in volume what they lose in a more protracted relationship, and the profits to the pharmaceutical industry soar into the billions. Psychotropic medication does normally modify the child's behavior, but so does a lobotomy. There is an argument that a child made tractable by drugs is more teachable. But so is a child whose behavior is modified without the use of drugs. No healthy child should be kept in a bubble of chemical-based emotional isolation during the years when the child is supposed to be growing up.

A Better Way

Essentially, there is little difference between a child's motives in the old, destructive behavior and in the Mother Teresa activities that win praise and friendships. If children don't get what they want through appropriate behavior, or don't know how to be appropriate, they learn to get it through other ways. By exactly the same process, parents can teach mature behaviors so that they don't have to be obnoxious to get a desired result. Consider the example of a child who cannot get along with other children, one of the most common reasons parents seek the help of a therapist.

Aggression, rudeness, and even violence can be viewed as terrible pathologies demanding heavy drugs and years of treatment, or they can be seen more simply for what they are: a child's unsuccessful attempts to connect with others.

Aggression, rudeness, and even violence can be viewed as terrible pathologies demanding heavy drugs and years of treatment, or they can be seen more simply for what they are: a child's unsuccessful attempts to connect with others. The child continues to act that way because the shrieks and tears of peers, or even a punch in the nose, are better than no response at all.

With guidance, any parent can show that child a better way to get a much higher quality of attention, and the enormously increased satisfaction and sense of self that go with it.

8

TAKING STOCK,
SETTING GOALS

◄◦————◦►

THE HARRISONS CAME into my office on one of those bitter, dark
March days when the aftermath of a late-winter storm had covered the
sidewalks with crackling ice, and the promise of spring seemed to be
on permanent hold. They were both about 40, and both professionals—he was a design engineer with a local electronics firm, and she was
just easing back into a career in nursing, working three days a week at
a local retirement community. They had come on a referral from
another family in the same town, and both greeted me with the eager-
ness one might reserve for a firefighter or the driver of a tow truck. It
was instantly clear that they viewed me as their potential savior, but it
was also apparent, beneath the warmth, that their mood matched the
climate.

"It's about Thomas," Mrs. Harrison said. She spoke with the focused
urgency of someone who had just put her quarter into the telescope

43

and wanted to share her view of some distant disaster before her time ran out. "We have two children, both boys, but it's Thomas who's driving us crazy." She turned her head briefly toward her husband, who raised his eyebrows and offered a worn smile in affirmation. "Thomas is the older—he's 6," she added. She paused a moment, as though the information she had just given me might be enough for a man of my reputation and insight to propose an immediate solution.

I wrote the number 6 on a pad beside Thomas's name. I asked, "How old is the other child?"

"Three," the husband answered. "Jeffrey."

"And Jeffrey doesn't seem to be a problem?"

They turned to each other again. I was familiar with the exchange: partly they were looking for agreement, but each also displayed the smallest hint of apprehension that the other might be harboring some dreadful, untold evidence of how their second seed was turning bad as well. When they both expressed a relieved no, indicating that Jeffrey was just fine, I said, "So, tell me about Thomas."

While some families will simply characterize a problem child's behavior problems rather than describe them—he's lazy, she's defiant, he's mean to his siblings, she can't get along with other kids—the Harrisons replied with a catalog of specific incidents. Thomas had cried and called his father a jerk because he wasn't allowed to stay up for the end of a ball game his family was watching on television—one of the Red Sox–Yankees play-offs for the World Series. He went into another tearful rage, for no apparent reason, when his mother said he had to go with her to the supermarket. He threw another fit when he was not allowed to go to a friend's house for a sleepover because it was the same evening as his mother's birthday. He liked to spend time on the family's sleep sofa in the den, and he became furious whenever his father folded it up for daytime use or when they had company. In these and other incidents of conflict, he got red in the face to the point where his father wondered if he was going to have a stroke.

There were other behavioral problems with daily routine. He didn't like to listen to instructions. He occasionally refused to get dressed to go to school, although he was always responsible about putting on the proper clothes for play. His brother and their cousins were quiet by nature, and Thomas liked to "zip things up," in his father's words, when he was with the other children, sometimes by engaging them in pushing and shouting matches, but more often in the form of rowdy play. He sometimes took toys away from his brother just to get a reaction and was similarly demanding of attention, though usually not in a negative way, from both of his parents.

Time-outs didn't seem to work when he behaved poorly, partly because a lot of his tantrums took place around bedtime and Thomas was smart enough to know that his parents weren't going to keep him up late just to teach him a lesson. Besides, the time-outs were in his bedroom. Associating the bedroom with punishment—and no matter how benign, time-out is a punishment—is just asking for more trouble at bedtime on days when he has not misbehaved. (Other good reasons not to use a bedroom for a time-out are discussed in Chapter 15.)

On the positive side, Thomas got along well with everyone in school, including his teacher. He was outgoing, and it was clear that his classmates looked at him as a dependable source of fun and excitement. This may seem puzzling, but in most cases, kids who are driving their par-

> In most cases, kids who are driving their parents crazy at home are just fine in kindergarten or elementary school.

The parents had no trouble understanding that the reason Thomas didn't like rules was also why he always wanted his own way: he wanted to be a big boy.

ents crazy at home are just fine in kindergarten or elementary school. This says two important things. First, the problem at home is not the symptom of some kind of psychological illness, as one might otherwise conclude based on the medical model, given that it can be turned on and off. And second, home and school are two different environments, and the child is getting two different sets of instruction on how to behave—further evidence in support of the learning model over the medical one. It is a rare child who is a pain to those around him in both settings—but even the exceptions are seldom likely to deserve a medical diagnosis for their immature behavior.

The differences in Thomas's case weren't just in school. At the beach he would frequently go up to other children his age and make nearly instant friends of strangers. The past summer he had adopted a family, introducing them to Jeffrey and his parents, and afterward, whenever Thomas appeared on the beach, they greeted him as one of their own.

By the end of that first meeting, I had heard enough that I was able to work with the parents in setting some specific goals for how Thomas's behavior could be improved. Here's the list:

1. Get Thomas to listen. This includes follow-up, so that when he is told to do something, he does it in a responsive, timely way.
2. Help Thomas find a reliable method of calming himself down and curbing the impulses that get him into trouble.
3. Help Thomas learn to get along with his brother all the time instead of just some of the time.

4. Stop the tantrums.
5. Stop the hitting and name-calling.

The Big Three

As I always do, I explained to the parents that their son needed to learn three things in order for any of these goals to be achieved. He had to learn that we live in a world in which we do not always get what we want. In that same world there are other people whose needs, feelings, and wishes have to be respected. And finally, he would have to learn self-control.

His mother pointed out that Thomas wasn't fond of the concept of rules, so it was agreed we would not use that word in our plan. In fact, I rarely speak of rules in my practice. My role in working with parents is not to act as a judge or referee in the game of growing up. It is merely to explain categories of behavior and offer advice on how they can be nurtured or eliminated. The parents had no trouble understanding that the reason Thomas didn't like rules was also why he always wanted his own way: he wanted to be a big boy. He got so upset when the sleep sofa was folded up because when he was allowed to use it as a bed, it was larger than the one he usually slept in, and he associated it with being accepted as a grown-up. Defiance in this and other areas was his way of saying he was a big boy. Nobody tells a big boy what to do, and only babies have to listen to Mom and Dad. I explained that the reason he got particularly angry when his parents had to dress him for school was that he viewed being dressed by his parents as a sign that they regarded him as an infant.

Thomas loved his grandmother, but he associated visits to her house with a body of rules equal to the federal penal code, and if there was one thing worse than being treated like a baby, it was being treated like a grandbaby. It was agreed that the Harrisons would enlist the grandmother, who they said was an intelligent, sensitive woman, in the task ahead.

Getting On Track

Even though we didn't call them rules, the list items included things that Thomas would not be able to do: no standing on the sofa or on the windowsill; no throwing things; no tantrums. The primary focus of the program, however, was on the dos, not on the don'ts.

Starting that day, the parents agreed to keep a diary, tracking three classes of behavior. They would list specific examples of sibling caring, which meant they would note every time Thomas was nice with his brother—that is, encouraging, inclusive, thoughtful, helpful, kindly, and so forth. They had already given me several examples of that type of behavior, so I knew these events would be plentiful. They would similarly track all instances of Mother Teresa behavior, the class of behavior indicative of his positive awareness of others: trying to please someone (e.g., listening); offering to assist in clearing the table or putting the dishes away; responding in a timely way, and without objections, to routine responsibilities such as getting ready for school or going to bed; and being helpful or loving with Mom and Dad. And finally they would record instances of taking disappointment calmly, the times when Thomas chose not to fly into a tearful rage when things did not go as he had hoped or wanted. I told them the diary should list six to ten examples, which we would review on their next weekly visit.

I also advised them to not confuse themselves in the meanwhile by reading any of the self-help books on parenting that encourage the very behaviors we were planning to end.

9

DEAR DIARIES:
TWO EXAMPLES

❦⟶❦

THIS CHAPTER ISN'T SO MUCH about what goes into the diary, which I hope by now is pretty clear, as it is about what comes out of it. Like the first session in which the parents and I create a record of the problem behaviors and set some specific goals for improvement, the diary records the process and establishes baselines for measuring progress.

Keeping the diary is important for another reason that is absolutely essential to the outcome. It provides a simple, reliable, and relatively painless method for changing the primary focus of the parents' inter-action with their child from negative to positive. Parents come to me in the first place because of everything that is going wrong. In every case they bring a list, sometimes on paper and sometimes in their heads, of the ways in which the problems present themselves. Those lists are appropriate and helpful—I can't imagine asking a parent what seems to be the problem and receiving only a shrug or a blank stare. But given that those lists of what's wrong are a road map to the chaos in their lives, it makes sense that the road map out of that chaos would point in exactly the opposite direction. Here is how a couple of families created and used their own road maps of the route from difficult to delightful.

Subsequent chapters offer more detailed information on how to put the maps to use.

Example One: Brother Bashing

Isaac, age 3, appeared to have taken a distinct disliking to his brother of 18 months. It hadn't always been that way. The second child, Aaron, was born just after Isaac had learned to walk and before he was old enough to speak whole sentences. His parents told me they had tried to share the excitement of their expectation with Isaac through the later months of the pregnancy. Although Isaac had picked up on their enthusiasm, he was still largely preoccupied with the process of emerging from his own infancy. But by the time Isaac was 2, he was becoming more aware of the stranger who had succeeded him on the changing table and was coming to view Aaron as a serious rival.

By the time the parents came to me for help, the tension had ripened into a variety of bad habits. There were still many occasions when Isaac treated his brother lovingly, but Aaron was now the same age Isaac had been at the time of the brother's birth, and with growing frequency their relationship was punctuated by poking, prodding, and punching. Isaac pulled his brother's hair and fought with him for Aaron's toys.

The parents had read several of the standard texts on child rearing, and they decided, as the books suggested, that Isaac's behavior was a jealous attempt to reclaim their full attention. So, whenever such an event took place, they dutifully picked Isaac up or hugged him, also as the books advised, assuring him that he was the sweetest, smartest, nicest little boy on the face of the earth.

I was not surprised to learn that this response, which had been recommended as an antidote to the bad behavior, proved instead to be an incentive to increasing its frequency. Isaac was getting the attention he wanted, but the parents were giving it to him at the wrong time and for the wrong reasons. It's a pretty simple concept, but when parents hear it for the first time, there is often a moment in which they appear to be overwhelmed by its common sense. "Wow," Isaac's father said, dazzled by this first glimpse of the obvious.

I described my program to the parents, and Isaac's mother agreed to keep a diary for the next thirty days. They continued with the same types of encouragement and reassurance as before, but now it was offered only in response to the mature behavior and never for the aggression. If Isaac helped his brother with his early walking, for example, she would say, "That's wonderful that you're being so caring. You're such a big boy, Isaac, and that's the kind of thing a big boy does."

Isaac delighted in the praise. "I'm a big boy," he would agree. And in short order he began looking about for new ways to prove just how big he was.

His mother would record the events as they occurred, and at around suppertime she'd sit down with Isaac, and sometimes with his father as well, to vividly recall the positive events of the day. "I'm so proud of you when you show me the ways you're growing up," she would tell him. Then as a reward, she would sit with him and read him a children's book. After the second day of this, Isaac recognized there would be a reward and began coming to these sessions with the book he wanted his mother to read to him that evening. The positive behaviors were small, but they quickly became more caring and more numerous.

Isaac started doing helpful things for his mother when he saw that she was about to begin a familiar household chore. In response to his little brother's request, he went to the refrigerator and poured him a glass of milk. The next day he did it again, but this time without being asked. He began playing with Aaron as a collaborator rather than a competitor. He delighted in finding ways to make his brother laugh, instead of cry.

At that point, the mother made a change in the way she related to the two children together. Whereas she had previously excluded Isaac from his little brother's bedtime ritual because she feared his response, she now began to include him. The three of them would lie together on the baby's bed, the mother rocking Aaron and singing softly to both of them, and Isaac lying beside her smiling or watching thoughtfully in contented silence.

The turnaround was quick and dramatic. Within a month the aggressive behavior so recently the norm was now a rarity, and by the end of the second month it had virtually ceased.

Another kind of turnaround took place that neither of the parents had contemplated. Their own attitude toward Isaac changed as his behavior improved. They no longer dreaded his interactions with Aaron, and their feelings of frustration and anger, until then largely unacknowledged, began to fade away as well. "For the first time in months," his mother said, "he's a delight to be with. We're having so much fun and pleasure again."

Example Two: Heaving and Howling

Taylor, age 4, was a little girl who seemed to be preparing for a career in either major-league baseball or grand opera. She threw things at her mother—toys, clothes, pillows, blocks, dirt, and, on at least one occasion, a moderately sized rock. She also threw tantrums, lying facedown on the floor in kicking fits and screaming at the top of her very large voice. Her mood shifts were violent and generally unpredictable, although they frequently occurred when one of her parents appeared to be planning to leave the house for any reason.

"She'll throw whatever she has in her hand," her mother told me. "Sometimes it's because something isn't going her way, but more often we can't even guess. Anger. Disgust. Who knows? The best part of our day together is when she's in bed and finally asleep. It's exhausting."

One characteristic of her rage appeared to be associated with a need for instant gratification. She was unable to take no for an answer to even the most unreasonable demand. If she asked for a glass of milk just before the family was about to sit down for supper, for example, her mother's response that she would have it in just a minute would be met with howls of protest. "I want a glass of milk! I want a glass of milk! I want a glass of milk!" Another feature was that her response followed a pattern, escalating to a pitch and volume of rage that permeated the house and stressed everyone in the family.

She had particular difficulty relating to her older sister, who was 7. When they did play together, it was always on Taylor's terms, and those terms could change in an instant. Soon game boards would be upset, toys would go flying, and she would sometimes try to physically push the larger girl out of the room.

"We may not sound like it, but we're a very affectionate family," Taylor's mother told me. "We hug each other a lot, and we like to show our feelings. But with Taylor, she'll accept a hug or a kiss when she thinks she's in control of the situation, but most of the time when she sees it coming, she'll stiffen up and push us away."

She was rude with strangers. Her family found themselves holding their collective breath, waiting in near dread for whatever she was going to do next. Whenever her mother took her into a supermarket, she

The positive behaviors were small, but they quickly became more caring and more numerous.

would drop to the floor in a screaming fit at the moment she sensed she was about to be placed in the shopping cart. Any journey out of the house was an ordeal. Even while screaming at full pitch, she could turn her body into instant dead weight, and she knew how to throw it around.

She would hit her sister out of the blue. One day they were in the tub together, and the older girl suddenly vented her feelings in a combination of frustration and despair. "Why are you so mean to me, Taylor?" she pleaded. "I try to be nice to you, and all you do is hit me and be mean."

Fast-forward to six weeks later. Taylor's mother has been keeping a diary, and here are some of the entries from the past couple of days:

"The first thing that comes to mind when I think of Taylor is that she is like a different child. If she has a request and I tell her I'm in the middle of something, she takes it in and says, 'OK, after you're finished, then.'

"She's 100 percent more affectionate. Now when she comes up to me, instead of throwing something or pushing me away, she'll give me a hug or a kiss—which she never did before in her life. Every morning for the last week, she comes into our bedroom to tap me on the shoulder and say, 'Good morning, Momma. Did you have a good sleep?' It's the same thing I ask her every morning, and now she's so eager to treat me the same way that she comes in to say it to me before I'm even awake.

"She still has her moments, but the difference is like night and day. Today she's a normal kid. If she starts to get upset or begins to scream, all I have to say to her is, 'Taylor, you know we don't scream.'

"And even if she does something that requires a time-out, she has developed a pattern of repeating whatever I've just said that warranted that response, like, 'We don't scream,' or 'We don't throw crayons.' I put her in the time-out chair, and she's very good and sits right there. She doesn't try to get up or run away. After the time is up, I'll turn to her and say, 'OK, you've been well behaved, so you can get up now.' She'll get up and repeat, 'Momma, we don't scream.' And I'll say, 'Yes, Taylor, that's right.'

"We're giving her the same amount of attention/affection/discipline as we did before, only now in a different way and with a far different result. I enter everything in the diary—the Mother Teresa behavior, handling disappointment calmly, the caring behavior—and as of last week, we started including the negative things and how we're dealing with them.

"When I use this method, she always gives me a hug and laughs and jumps up and down, saying, 'I remember, I remember.' Today she was playing with something, and entirely on her own, she said, 'Momma, do you remember yesterday when I was being such a big girl and helped you fold the napkins?' And I said, 'Yes, Taylor, I do remember, and I think it's wonderful that you're being such a big girl.'

"Before we started, I didn't praise her often—first because there was so little to praise, and second because she took praise so poorly. But once we began, I looked for things to praise like a prospector after gold, and when I found something, I'd jump all over it. 'Taylor, that's so-o-o good!' Despite her initial resistance, she is far more affectionate in return—all because I'm giving her the praise.

"It's hard to give affection when you know it's going to be rejected— even for a parent. It was getting to be especially difficult for her sister. But that's another milestone for how far we've all come. The other day I overheard them as they were playing together. Taylor has pretty much lost her old bossiness and impatience, and they were getting along at a real level of give-and-take. 'Gee, Taylor,' her sister said, 'You're pretty fun when you're not being mean to me.' Taylor started to answer in agreement, but before she said much, her sister called to me in the kitchen: 'Ma, is Taylor learning to be more fun?'

"Taylor answered for me. 'Yes,' she said, 'I'm learning to be a big girl.'"

10

HANDLING
DISAPPOINTMENT

WHENEVER PARENTS COME to me with stories of their child's low tolerance for frustration, the focus is usually on the impact this lack of control has on the rest of the family. Their 5-year-old creates a scene, scares or bullies his little sister, picks a fight with an older brother, whines, cries, strikes out, throws things, and generally disturbs the peace of the household. Behind those external manifestations, however, most parents share a deeper concern for the implications this type of behavior has for the child's ability to grow, socialize, assimilate experience, and learn from failures.

They are right to worry. Every experience in life, good or bad, contains a lesson. The more a child's energy is spent in anger at his or her limitations—in body skills, in managing time, in self-sufficiency, in doing whatever gives amusement, stimulation, or pleasure—the less of that child's energy is available to the process of learning anything use-

The more a child's energy is spent in anger at his or her limitations—in body skills, in managing time, in self-sufficiency, in doing whatever gives amusement, stimulation, or pleasure—the less of that child's energy is available to the process of learning anything useful from those experiences. It is just as hard for children to put their disappointments to use when they are made angry by their frustration as it is for adults—and can be even harder. But children who have been taught to take disappointment calmly have a tremendous advantage over those who have not. They are in a much better position to grow from their experiences. By itself, the calm response is a sign of maturity that should inspire encouragement and trust. And calm children are much more fun to be with than children who respond to disappointment by exploding on contact.

Taking Note of Taking It Well

Here are some commonplace examples of calm behavior as recorded by parents and shared with me the following week. The diary entry is in italics at the end of each story.

"We dropped Morgan at school. Mary wanted to go in with us to see the place where her older brother spent the day, but we were running late, and I told her we would have to wait. I made it clear that I thought her request was reasonable, and I said I was looking forward to sharing the experience with her some other time. When I returned to the car, I said, 'Mary, I know you really wanted to go inside today, and you acted like a big girl when Mommy said not today. I'm very proud of you.' It was obvious that my praise was more important to her than getting her way."

Was good about not going in with me to Morgan's classroom.

"There is a vending machine in the lobby outside the doctor's office, and Kevin remembered it from prior visits. Today when we entered the building, he ran up to the machine and said he wanted some candy. The elevator door was about to close, and I said we didn't want to keep the doctor waiting. Kevin weighed his choices for a moment and then followed me into the elevator. It turned out that one of the doctor's office staff was on her way up as well, and she recognized us from previous visits. 'My, Kevin,' she said, 'you certainly are a grown-up boy. I'm sure your mother is very proud of you.' Kevin was delighted, and when he smiled down at his shoes, I suddenly had the comic thought that Dr. Azerrad had put the woman up to saying what she did. 'Yes,' I assured them both, 'I certainly am.'"

Got on elevator without a fuss after asking for candy on doctor visit.

"Freddie has just learned to ride his tricycle, and he loves to pedal it up and down the sidewalk in front of the house. Because the experience is still new to him, I walk along beside him on these trips. One reason is to keep him from falling off, and another is that I can't rely on him to stay on our property, especially when the first and second graders in the house next to us are riding their own bicycles on the street. Today, when the neighbor kids got off the school bus, Freddie was watching at our door, and he asked if he could go outside. I was on a long-distance call with a friend, and because I didn't want to cut her off, I told him he'd have to wait. He stood patiently at the screen door, watching the older kids as they played without him. When one of them called over asking him to join them, he called back that he'd be there 'in a while' but that he had to wait for his mommy. It was another ten minutes before I got off the line, but he never complained. I told him how proud I was that he was such a grown-up boy."

Waited patiently to go outside.

"We were at the municipal pool, and in the past Adam has often made a ruckus when it was time to leave. I have explained that we have to be home when his older sister gets off the bus. Today he didn't make a fuss and left the pool as soon as I told him it was time to go."

Left pool nicely.

"On Tuesday afternoons we go to story time at the local library, and at the end of the reading the staff serves cookies and soft drinks. Today there were more kids than usual, and they ran out of lemonade, which is Ella's favorite. There is a corner store about a block from the library, but it took about ten minutes for one of the parents to return with a carton for the kids who didn't get any. Meanwhile, a couple of the other kids started to cry. Ella held on to her cookie and waited. She talked with some of the other children about the story they had just heard, but one eye was on the door. When the other mother returned, Ella was first in line, but she stood aside

and let the two younger kids who had been crying go ahead of her. When we were outside, I told her I was very, very proud."
Was patient about lemonade and let other kids go first.

"Our pediatrician is pretty punctual in the early part of the day, but his schedule can get away from him, and some afternoons we have long waits. Tammy's appointment today was at three, but it was almost four before the doctor finally got to see her. For the entire wait, she sat patiently in her chair at a small play table in one corner of the waiting room. Some of the time she drew in a coloring book or read from a dog-eared edition of Dr. Seuss. She struck up a conversation with a couple of other kids who were ahead of us and were a lot less patient about the wait than Tammy. I told her she was a very grown-up girl to be so well behaved."
Waited patiently through long delay in Dr. Friesen's office.

"Lisa's best friend in day care is Nancy, and her mother and I sometimes trade off babysitting each other's kids. On a couple of occasions they have slept over at one or the other's house. For three days Lisa had been looking forward to spending the whole day at Nancy's house on Saturday, but that morning her mother called me to say a family situation had arisen and they had to cancel. Lisa had her toys all packed when I had to break the news, and I expected the worst. To my surprise, instead of throwing a tantrum, she thought for a moment and then asked if Nancy and her mother were OK. I told her they were, and she looked relieved. 'OK,' she said, 'maybe next weekend.' I told her I thought she was the best, most grown-up girl in the world."
Was thoughtful and calm about not going to Nancy's.

Accentuating the Positive

It occurs to me that my putting these examples on paper risks creating a false impression. Although each account illustrates an occasion for reinforcing the kind of behavior this book is written to nurture, it would be a mistake to assume that in just one week these former terrors have given up their earlier ways to live in total harmony with the world. That's not the case with any of them. The same day she was so good about handling her disappointment over visiting her brother's classroom, little Mary threw a fit over an entirely different disappointment while shopping with her mother in the supermarket. Kevin, Freddie, Adam, Ella, Tammy, and Lisa also performed equally heinous crimes against humanity on the very days they exhibited the exemplary behaviors cited here.

> The parts of their day that these children will all remember the longest are the ones that earned them the most positive attention and reinforcement from their parents.

The point of all these stories is that the parts of their day that these children will all remember the longest are the ones that earned them the most positive attention and reinforcement from their parents. And it is that type of behavior, not the mopes or hissy fits or tantrums, that they now have the greatest incentive to repeat.

Other Examples of Diary Notations on Taking Disappointment Calmly

Broke bicycle chain and missed ride; asked how to fix it.
Reacted calmly when Dad brought home the wrong video.

Quickly recovered from not being invited to Jane's birthday party.
Cried at death of pet hamster but then consoled little sister.
Frustrated at spelling, resolved to study harder.
Missed school aquarium trip due to flu; asked if we'd take him someday.
Looked for alternatives when his favorite TV show was cancelled.
Lost ice cream money through hole in pocket; asked me to sew it up.

11

MOTHER TERESA BEHAVIORS

ONE OF MY FAVORITE STORIES about Mother Teresa concerns a wealthy woman who approached this self-sacrificing and universally admired nun and asked her how it was possible to follow in her footsteps: "You have gone to faraway Calcutta, where you have given your life in service to the neediest and most hopeless people on the planet, offering more love and solace in their final days and hours than many of them experience in a lifetime. How can any of the rest of us come close to that kind of nobility? We live in the secular world, with responsibilities and families and the need to earn a living. How can I do anything at all like what you have done without throwing away everything I have worked for and betraying everyone who depends on me right here at home?"

Mother Teresa's answer was, "Find your own Calcutta."

Just to be clear, this wasn't about geography. Mother Teresa wasn't necessarily referring to a potential equivalent to the slums of Haiti or Johannesburg or to the flood-ravaged towns of Louisiana—although these popular mission sites offer fertile opportunities for sacrifice, and the potential for return in satisfaction, equal to what she found in India. What she was saying was that human need is everywhere: for love, comfort, empathy, kindness, caring. We don't need to travel to the other side of the world to be of use, to offer the gifts that define us and make us whole.

> We don't need to travel to the other side of the world to be of use, to offer the gifts that define us and make us whole.

Beginning at Home

These days, when we hear that "charity begins at home," as often as not it is said as an ironic comment on people who put their own interests ahead of the common good. But in its original, noble sense, it is still as true as ever. And for most of us, home is where these qualities of caring are learned and first put to use. Two thousand years ago, a Jewish philosopher described a similar process when he cited the Maker's covenant with his children on Earth. "God says," Hillel told us, "'If you come to my house, I will come to yours.'"

Here are some examples of Mother Teresa behaviors in children, first as observed in context by their parents and then, in italics, as they were recorded in the family's diary.

"I was putting the girls to bed, and after reading them a story in their room, I said to them, 'Mommy is tired, Daddy and I have both been working very hard, and tonight I need you to help us by going to sleep without a fuss.' I kissed them both and tucked them in. They shut their eyes tight and snuggled down in their beds with the obvious intention of getting to sleep as soon as possible. I turned out the light and never heard another sound from them until morning."

Went to sleep without a fuss "to help Mommy."

"We have a big backyard, and in the warm months I spend a lot of time in the garden. Chris turned 2 this spring, and one of his birthday presents was a little patch of soil among the flowers that he could call his own. Like his mother, he loves playing in the dirt, and it's a way for me to keep an eye on him while I work. He's very interested in the things I plant, and he putters happily along beside me with his pail and shovel. The only drawback is that his clothes have to be washed after every session. I undress him as soon as we get back inside, and while he puts on a fresh shirt and pants, I take the soiled clothes over to the laundry basket.

"Yesterday I got as far as handing him his new clothes when the phone rang, so I dropped the dirty clothes on the floor and crossed the kitchen to answer it. A moment later, I looked over to check on him. Chris had finished redressing, and he bent down to pick up the clothes from the floor and walked them over to the hamper, just as I usually do. I interrupted the phone call to tell him what a nice thing that was to do. He beamed in response and said, 'I help you, Mommy.'"

Chris dressed himself and put his clothing in the hamper.

"Last Tuesday night we both had meetings: my wife is a library trustee, and I belong to a men's group at our church. We ate supper in a hurry, and the babysitter arrived from next door before we had time to clear the dishes. We apologized for the way the house looked, said goodnight to Anna, and rushed to our cars. Anna's 6, which meant she would be in bed by the time we got home at nine.

"I returned first, and just as I was about to pay the sitter, I noticed that the dinner table had been cleared, the kitchen was picked up, and the dishes were in the washer. The deal with our sitter is that on school nights all she has to do is put Anna to bed on time. 'Whoa,' I said, feeling suddenly guilty, 'you're not supposed to do that. What about your homework?'

"She laughed and told me, 'I did it while Anna picked up. It was all her idea, and she started doing it without saying a word. Don't tell my mother and father about this: if they remember what I was like at 6, they'll want to trade kids.'

"We were so proud of my daughter that we both wanted to wake her up just to tell her so. But we decided to wait until morning."
Cleared table, did dishes by herself.

"David is at an age where he likes to dress himself without any interference from his parents, so I was surprised last Saturday morning when he thanked me for giving him a hand as he struggled to put on his trousers. He knew I was going to clean the house for a family cookout that afternoon, and when I commented on how nice it was for him to thank me, he said, 'You said you have a lot to do today, and I got dressed to help you, Mommy.'"
Thanks for help dressing; offered to help clean house.

"We went up to New Hampshire on a family camping trip last weekend, and on the first night, my husband put a couple of recliners out in a field so he and Frannie, 5, could lie back and watch the stars come out. We spend a lot of time with the kids together, but we also make an effort to give them both some one-on-one, so I stayed back at the tent, cleaning up after supper and putting Frannie's brother Eric, 3, into his bed. When they both came back from the field, I was sitting by the lantern reading a book, and I asked Frannie what they had seen. 'We saw two planets—Daddy thinks they're Mars and Venus. We saw the Milky Way. Did you know the Milky Way is our galaxy?'

"'Isn't that wonderful,' I answered. 'I'm surprised you're back so soon. Were there mosquitoes?'

"Frannie came over and took my hand. 'No,' she said, 'we came back so I could take you out to see the Big Dipper. One of the points in the handle is actually a double star, a bright one and a dim one right next to each other, and Daddy says they're a test of vision for people who live in the desert. I can see them, and I wanted to point them out so you can see them too.'"
Pointed out stars in Big Dipper.

"Our cat, Archie, is 18, which means we've had him almost four times longer than we've had Charlie, our youngest child. Archie has a hard time walking, and he has had several small accidents in the living room. As long as he wasn't in pain, I would never put a pet to sleep, but I finally decided it was time for a trip to the vet for some advice and perhaps some medicine. Charlie saw that I was anxious, and he asked if Archie was about to die. 'Not yet,' I assured him, 'but he's very old, and we have to expect that to happen sometime soon.'

"The vet said Archie was dehydrated and gave him some fluids under the skin. Charlie held the cat in his lap on the way back home, and I could tell from time to time that he was giving me quick glances to determine my state of mind. Finally he said, 'You got Archie way back when you were in college?' The story of how

Even in adult relationships, if a small kindness happens to be bracketed by something less positive or that needs an immediate response, it's often overlooked or soon forgotten.

I had found him in a shelter for strays was a part of the family lore, and Charlie wasn't so much asking as assuring me that he knew how important the little cat had been in my life even back before he was born.

"We got back to our house, and as I turned off the engine, Charlie looked over at me once again, and this time he caught my eye and held it. 'No matter what happens,' he said, 'I know that Archie is going to be all right.'

"It was one of the kindest reassurances I've ever heard."
Said Archie would be OK.

Saints, Preserve Us

Because Mother Teresa behavior is usually a lot quieter than its opposite, it is easy to miss. Even in adult relationships, if a small kindness happens to be bracketed by something less positive or that needs an immediate response, it's often overlooked or soon forgotten. Whenever I hear about Mother Teresa behaviors like the examples cited in this chapter, it's tempting to believe that the little angels who performed these good deeds may be transported directly to their reward in heaven. Then I remind myself of why the parents are in my office. They haven't sought me out because everything is as wonderful as their last story, but because their kids are driving them nuts.

Other Examples of Diary Notations on Mother Teresa Behaviors

Helped bring Dana her breakfast.

At baby sister's bedtime brought me her bottle from the shelf.

Helped put the groceries away.

Asked if she could help make cookies for Nancy's mom, who is sick.

Swept kitchen after dinner.

Ran ahead to hold door for me when my arms were full of bags and boxes.

Prayed for Grammie, who is having eye surgery, at dinner table.

Called her friend Claire to say she was glad they got a new dog.

Asked me if a lady with one item could go ahead of us at the store.

Put three M&Ms under his brother's dinner plate.

12

RIVALRY REVERSED: SIBLING CARING

AN OLD SPANISH PROVERB counsels, To have a friend, be a friend. You've heard variations on it all your life: To be loved, be loving; You get what you give; and the usually negative corollary, What goes around comes around. It all started with the philosopher Hillel, who said, "What is hateful to you, do not do to your neighbor." Most of us know this as the Golden Rule, with its advice about doing unto others. In any family of more than one child, the greatest amount of "doing unto" activity, for good and bad, takes place among or between siblings.

In a word-association test, a guaranteed response to *sibling* is *rivalry*. Outside of psychology, it's unusual to hear the first word used without the second. Except for families with only one child, a primary focus of almost every problem brought to me by worried parents is the relationship between the children. The first child excludes and belittles a younger brother. The second child tattles on his older brother and picks on his baby sister. Kids hog toys, push and punch in play, lie, shun, steal.

Years ago, at a cocktail party, I met a woman with twins. When I politely asked if double births ran in her family, she said, "Yes, I had a twin brother." I responded to her use of the past tense with an inadvertent look of sympathetic acknowledgement, whereupon she added, "When we were 8, he was teasing me, and I pushed him out of a second-floor window."

I*n a word-association test, a guaranteed response to *sibling* is *rivalry*.

I was astonished, not just at the revelation but at the way she had said it, with the matter-of-fact, flat affect of someone reading an eye chart. "My God," I said, "what a terrible accident."

"It wasn't an accident," she corrected patiently, and I began to realize that the reason for her tone was that she had told this story so many times before. Each time, her audience had done what I did: found an excuse for what she had just revealed, glossed it over, changed the unimaginable into something they could deal with. She continued, "It would have been an accident if he just fell. But he didn't just fall; I pushed him." And then, in case there were any doubt left that I had got the message, she stated, "It was murder."

Guarding the Door

The book of Genesis is equally straightforward about the first murder in the new creation. When God favored the offering by Abel over that of his older brother, Cain flew into a rage. Seeing this, God gave Cain a little pep talk. "If you do well, will you not be accepted? And if you do not do well, sin is couching at the door; its desire is for you, but you must master it."

That's excellent advice, even if Cain ignored it. Psychologists aren't in the business of evaluating the human condition in terms of sin and salvation, but if sin equates with destructive behavior and salvation lies in the other direction, then at least in that one regard most of us tend to be on the side of God. One of the most satisfying parts of my work with families in crisis is helping them to restructure sibling relationships that have gone awry. It means replacing selfishness with sharing, destruct with construct, and jealousy with shared pride. At its most fundamental level, it means replacing rivalry with caring.

Here are some examples of sibling caring as described to me by parents, followed by the words, in italics, they used to note it in their diary.

"Jack and Hannah both like Chinese checkers, but they play by different rules. Jack goes by the directions on the box, while his younger sister likes to make things up as they go along. Whenever they sat down to play, Hannah would follow Jack's rules for the first few moves, but then she'd start to take two turns at a time or jump into spaces that weren't allowed—and Jack would blow up. He'd grab her hand to stop the play, tell her she was stupid and a little baby, and end up by throwing the game board onto the floor. I'd make him clean it up, but still I'd find marbles down the heating duct, behind the sofa, and all over the house.

"It was about a month since their last game. This past Wednesday Hannah finally got up her nerve to ask again if he wanted to play. As I braced myself for the inevitable explosion, I had an idea: I suggested they play one game by Hannah's rules and then another one by Jack's. It took a lot of self-control, especially by Jack. But even though he started out being patient only because he knew he would get his way later, after a few minutes I saw a change. Instead of dealing with her as a deadly rival, he started treating his sister like the little girl she is, and the strained patience gave way to a real interest in helping her to learn the game. He was being nice to her because it felt good to be a big brother."

Was patient and sharing with Hannah in Chinese checkers.

"On our way back from the movies, I found a roll of Life Savers in the glove compartment and passed them around the car. When Jane, 5, asked for another one, her brother Mark, 6, immediately asked for seconds as well. I gave the remainder of the pack to Jane and told her she could be in charge of them as long as she promised to share equally with Mark. I could hear them both crunching away, so I repeated what I had said. A moment later, Mark asked for another.

"There were only three Life Savers left, and as soon as Jane gave one to Mark, she looked at the other two and realized she was going to be on the losing end of the unequal division. She put one in her mouth and looked down a little pensively at the last one in her hand. Mark chewed as fast as ever, and in less than a minute he demanded the last piece of candy. Jane passed it to him without a murmur, and after Mark had crunched that one up as well, he smirked triumphantly and announced, 'I got four. I got the most.'

"In the rearview mirror, I saw Jane turn to her brother, and even though it was dark, I could see the tip of her tongue. I told her she had done the right thing in sharing, and I was proud of her, but I wasn't proud of how her brother was teasing her, or how she answered by sticking out her tongue. 'I wasn't,' she said. 'I was showing him how I made mine last by not chewing.'"

Shared Life Savers without complaining.

"Wendy and her little sister Tammy are both preschoolers. About three mornings a week Wendy visits a friend three doors away, and her friend plays at our house in the afternoon. It's a trade-off with the mother.

"Tammy usually throws a tantrum when Wendy leaves for her morning visits, and she's obnoxious in the afternoon, demanding attention, disrupting play, screaming and crying when she doesn't get her way. Wendy and her friend are both 5, and Tammy is 18 months younger; she feels excluded to begin with, and her behavior widens the gap. But yesterday, things changed.

"In the morning, just before Wendy left, she was upstairs with her little sister. It didn't occur to me to ask what they were talking about, but when she left, Tammy called good-bye to her, and for the first time in weeks she didn't set up a howl as soon as her sister walked out the door. That afternoon, I was impressed with how well Tammy was behaving. They played hopscotch in the driveway, which Tammy likes because she considers it a big girl's game.

"Later I asked Wendy what she had been talking about with her sister in the morning. She said she knew how it felt to be left out, so she told her it was Tammy's turn to decide that afternoon's activity. When I said that was a nice thing for her to have done, she answered, 'I wanted her to feel better.'"
Considered Tammy's feelings and included her in play.

"We spent the past weekend at Grandma's house. David, 5, brought along his coloring book, but Michael, who is two years older, left his at home because Grandma lives in the country and he said he was going to spend all his time outdoors. But despite a good forecast, it rained all day Saturday. We don't let the kids watch television on these visits, and Michael was going nuts.

"It was David who solved the problem. Although he is usually very protective of his property, especially from his older brother, he asked Michael if he wanted to share his coloring book. At first Michael wasn't sure, but David said they could work beside each other on opposite pages and then Grandma would decide which one was best. Of course, with Grandma making them both feel like geniuses, they had a wonderful day."

Shared coloring book.

"On Harry's first day of school, he finally got his wish of boarding the same yellow school bus as his sister Kaitlin, who is just starting the third grade. He was excited about the adventure, but as we all walked to the bus stop, it was obvious he was also very apprehensive, not just about the ride but about the whole new day ahead. For weeks I had worked hard to reassure him, but now any control of the situation was about to leave my hands. He was shaky, and I was a total wreck.

"The bus arrived, the double door popped open, there were last-minute hugs, and Kaitlin pushed little Harry before her up the steps. She knew almost everyone on the bus, and they greeted her with a cheer—on the first day, I assume the same thing happened at almost every stop. Then I heard Kaitlin yell above the noise, 'This is my little brother Harry. It's his first day of school.' And there was a second cheer, every bit as raucous as the first, as the doors snapped shut. I knew Harry was off to a good start."

Introduced Harry on the school bus.

Beyond Sweetness and Light

I have been a lifelong fan of the old comic W. C. Fields, and I can just imagine what his reaction would have been to these examples of sibling caring. "My, my," he would probably say, strumming his fingers across the strings of an invisible harp and rolling his eyes to heaven, "what a felicitous tale, what a heartwarming opus." Like their parents and like me, Fields knew that whenever a kid (or almost anyone, for that matter) does something nice, there's another side to the coin. The week before Jack played Chinese checkers successfully with his little sister, for example, he had caused an overflow that brought down the kitchen ceiling by flushing Hannah's dolly clothing in the upstairs toilet. Two days after her stoical generosity with the Life Savers, little Jane scribbled with a green crayon all over her brother's homework. And so on.

The thing to remember is that home is where our children learn behavior patterns that can last a lifetime, and sibling relationships are potent predictors for the way our offspring eventually will relate to the entire world. For good or bad, parental attentiveness, encouragement, and guidance have a profound influence on how children get along with each other.

> Home is where our children learn behavior patterns that can last a lifetime, and sibling relationships are potent predictors for the way our offspring eventually will relate to the entire world.

Other Examples of Diary Notations on Sibling Caring
Asked Mom to help him buy a card for sister's birthday.
Praised younger brother's report card.
Told her little sister she looked cute in her new dress.
Wished big brother luck in Little League game.
Let younger sister borrow hair clip.
Picked brother as partner in three-legged race.
Defended sister in name-calling by neighbor children.

13

IT'S GROWN-UP TO CARE
ABOUT OTHERS

AMONG THE LEAST ACKNOWLEDGED, most overlooked quali-
ties of maturity are genuine sensitivity and caring for others—sibling
caring, Mother Teresa behavior, and taking disappointment calmly. We
hear a lot, maybe too much, in the media about "sensitivity," "emotional bonding," and the like, for people who are made to worry that
maybe they don't have them. Promoters who develop sensitivity-
training techniques have a field day with the subject because it's so
abstract that it can mean whatever they want it to mean. It can give rise
to opportunities for "talking it out," hours of therapy to set emotions
free, and "getting in touch with your feelings" and the feelings of others. It has become a lucrative occupation for the variety of advisers who
claim to lead men and women to learn how to be sensitive.

Sometimes these self-help programs and associated forms of therapy work, but often they don't. Regardless, no parents want to believe

that what the future holds for their children is a sense of emotional incapacity that has to be remedied by self-anointed specialists in social and psychological correctness. They want their children to learn to care for others as part of the normal process of growing up.

Unfortunately, many parents never realize that the kind of positive caring behavior that they hope their child will eventually learn is entirely teachable at a young age, as are all the other behaviors on which they place a high value.

Long-Term Dividends

People who care about others always have friends, regardless of their age. Caring children always have friends. So do caring adults. They have a good self-image. They know they do things that others think are worthwhile. Responsible children or adults care about the effect of their actions on other people. Other people, in turn, recognize this quality and trust them. This sensitivity to how our behavior affects others is a big part of what Dr. Daniel Goleman calls emotional intelligence.

The bonds of love between parents and children that flourish in an atmosphere of praise, in environments that feel good, are extended in later years to friends, to spouses, and to children.

In a country in which half of all marriages end in divorce, the most frequently cited grounds for termination are incompatibility, cruelty, and irreconcilable differences. Often these phrases of the law simply define a lack of caring or sensitivity. In most cases, the real cause of the divorce is that it is difficult for one or both of the partners to show or even to feel genuine bonds of affection for others.

Even when a husband and wife do "care," they might never have learned how to give and take, how to recognize and accept caring behavior when it's being shown—just as some parents are blind or deaf to quiet behaviors in their children.

It is far too common in our world to view things negatively. Negative scanning leads parents to see only what is wrong with a child's behavior and to ignore or take for granted what is right. We are confronted again by the model for life that is focused on

> The bonds of love between parents and children that flourish in an atmosphere of praise, in environments that feel good, are extended in later years to friends, to spouses, and to children.

disease and problems, rather than on health and practical, natural solutions to the challenges of living.

You can teach your children to be caring. You can take a child who seems to have little sense of what caring about others means, or why it is useful, and build in that child a foundation for happiness that is among the most significant aspects of being truly grown-up.

The actions that signify caring in our society are different for different people. Frequently between adults—married or committed couples, in particular—caring behavior can be a lot of small things they do for each other. Dr. Richard Stuart, who works with couples who have marital problems, has a system of "caring days" in which couples make an effort to build a good, caring relationship by doing just those little things that signify caring to each spouse.

We can build this same attribute of adulthood in our children by teaching them to be caring when they are young. It's a matter of creating that positive feeling of self-worth in them, so that they are easily able to build a sense of self-worth in others.

We call it "thoughtfulness," an important caring behavior that has wide implications in the grown-up world, where the reward for a thoughtful, caring response to others is close bonds between friends and associates, between spouses, and with one's children.

More "Valuable" than "Cute"

Whenever a child does something thoughtful spontaneously, an adult response is often to say, "Isn't that cute!" But it is more than cute, and we should heavily praise a child who calls a sick friend to see how he is, or who tells another that she's really sorry she can't come over but to be sure to call again tomorrow. Sharing is thoughtful, a gesture such as picking flowers for Mother or any of the little things children do that show they are not just thinking of themselves and are truly sensitive to the feelings and needs of others. Sibling caring is a part of the natural bond, but it is the parent who sees this and other caring behaviors and who nurtures them.

Negative scanning leads parents to see only what is wrong with a child's behavior and to ignore or take for granted what is right.

We teach children with praise, by labeling the many different positive actions as valuable. Whether or not you are yourself especially caring or thoughtful, it's part of the job of being a parent to teach your children what it means and how to do it. Doing so is a lot less expensive than raising children who don't know how to care and end up as adults who search for answers about how to make people like them or how to express what they feel for others.

One couple told me that a teacher had observed that their son, Rick, was insensitive to the feelings of his fifth-grade classmates. In an attempt to be funny, he would make comments such as, "You look like a monkey," or, "You can only play backstop" to a heavy boy during a recess baseball game. If the other kids laugh at his insensitive remarks, he gains a slight feeling of self-worth. When he finds fault with other children, he increases his own feelings of self-worth at their expense, by making them look inferior. He characterizes others in a negative way to find a basis for balancing his own shortcomings.

In an attempt to change this behavior, his parents tried reasoning with him. They asked him how he would feel if the shoe were on the other foot and people said those kinds of things about him. They asked him again and again why he said the things that hurt his classmates, but to no avail. "It's as if he doesn't hear us," his mother told me. "He only hears those embarrassed laughs he gets from the other kids—sometimes even from kids he's done it to in the past."

It wasn't all that important to Rick that what he did made his classmates uncomfortable, even though they might have laughed. What was important to him was that his jibes got him a lot of attention.

Seize the Teachable Moment

The way to teach Rick more sensitive behavior is not to talk about it, because the criticism inherent in recounting what he has done wrong is a guarantee that he won't be listening; it's a nonteachable moment. A far more effective way of reaching Rick is a brief, immediate reprimand: "I don't like what I hear. I don't want you to talk that way to anyone." This tells him, without discussion, that his behavior is not appropriate.

Because most of Rick's unkind comments were made in school, I encouraged his parents to enlist Rick's teacher in using this corrective technique. The teacher was glad to oblige.

The way more sensitive behavior is taught is the same way that anything else is taught: through praise, communication of values in the teachable moment following praise, and an extra reward in the form of enjoyable time. Praise for the smallest incidents that show sensitivity, whether or not Rick really feels caring, has to take place at home. These incidents could include a moment of sharing, a comment that actually builds up another child instead of having the opposite effect, a gesture—perhaps even just a smile—that shows Rick is thinking of the other person. Mother Teresa behavior toward his classmates indicates both emotional intelligence and emotional maturity.

In teaching caring behavior, we build self-esteem, and if children feel good about themselves, they find it far easier to care about the feelings of their friends. Caring behavior in childhood reaches years into the future.

Parents can teach caring by recognizing it and making it as valuable to the child as it is to them. It is an essential lesson in becoming grown-up, and the ability to reach out and respond to others with sensitivity and understanding is something even the youngest child can begin to develop as a positive behavior that will last a lifetime.

14

THREE STEPS TO
SELF-CONTROL

YOU MAY BE FAMILIAR with the simplistic formula for a college lecture: first you tell them what you're going to tell them; then you tell them; then you tell them what you told them. Teaching children self-control, which is one of the most essential responsibilities of parenthood, follows something like that same three-step process. Here, the sequence is external control, verbal control, self-control.

Step One: External Control

The first step, external control, is a form of truth-and-consequences in which the parent does what the child is not yet able to do independently. The truth part is when the parent names the specific unacceptable behavior, with an admonition: "We do not throw blocks." "We do not call people names." "We do not draw on the wall." The consequence is usually referred to as a time-out, which involves placing the child in a chair facing a blank wall in a setting where external stimuli are minimized. This means no conversation; no television; no reading, playing, or drawing. Consider the alternatives: if the payoff for bad behavior is parental attention or some other form of gratification that the child would not get otherwise, even if it's extremely negative, that response becomes an incentive to engage in more of the same unacceptable actions.

Moviemakers will sometimes test a story line by filming alternative endings to see which one works best with an audience. We'll have more about time-outs in the following chapter, but in order to understand this first step in teaching self-control, let's look at alternative endings to a familiar domestic scenario.

In this true story, Ralph, 3, hears the familiar "buy me" chime from the Good Humor truck and excitedly runs into the kitchen. "Mommy, the ice cream man!" Mommy is in the midst of preparing supper, and she answers, "We're going to eat in just ten minutes, Ralph." The little boy merely stares at her in astonished incomprehension. The bell from the truck, which now is apparently parked under the elm tree right in front of their house, rings yet again. "Mommy," he repeats, this time the excitement giving way to anguish, "the *ice cream man!*" It is a moment that Pavlov would have savored. The mother drops to her knees to comfort him with a sympathetic hug. "Sweetie pie, Mommy has ice cream in the freezer, and we're going to have it for dessert." In response, little Ralph tries pushing her away, and in his panic to liberate himself (probably so he can run outside to try negotiating with the driver for a freebie), he smacks his mother's face with his elbow—wham! Mothers are used to getting accidentally pummeled, but to a boy of 3, punching Mommy in the face can lead to the same dreadful result whether he meant it or not, and he knows he has to create a diversion. He tilts his head back and howls. Mommy says, "It's all right, Ralphie." He keeps on howling anyway. Mommy draws back to regard her screaming son, ready to give him further assurances that he didn't really hurt her, when in among the gibberish, shrieks, and ululating she hears a familiar word: "Popsicle!" Either her son has lost track of his fear of reprisal, or he is deliberately changing the subject.

Several choices confront the mother at this juncture. She can continue to hug Ralph, hum to him, soothe him with "there, there"s, and wipe his cascading tears until he stops—which, if he's smart, will be never. She can yell back at him, try to snap some sense into him, and perhaps even burst into tears, guaranteed to produce the same result as choice one, and proving to Ralph that if this type of behavior is OK in an adult, he can keep on using it indefinitely. Third, she can lock him briefly in the bathroom while she goes outside and shoots the Good Humor man for parking in front of the house just before suppertime.

Time-out is a serious consequence and should be used sparingly, for only the most serious behaviors.

The last choice makes the most sense, but the correct answer is four, which is as follows. Mommy says, "We do not scream and yell." She then carefully picks Ralph up, takes him to wherever she keeps the time-out chair, seats him gently but firmly in it, and quietly withdraws to just a few feet away. Ralph can keep on howling, but despite the short distance to his mother it will quickly become apparent to him that he has lost his audience, and therefore his motive, and he shouldn't keep it up for long. So, external control is accompanied by verbal control (the concisely stated "We do not . . . ") and sometimes physical control—but the latter only to the extent of enforcing the time-out or intervening in harmful or destructive behavior. Time-out is a serious consequence and should be used sparingly, for only the most serious behaviors. It should never be employed in the presence of visitors or nonfamily or in any other location than the home.

Step Two: Verbal Control

In the second step, which is just verbal control without the time-out, words alone are enough to deter the unwanted behavior. In fact, the "verbal" part may be in the form of body language—just a positive facial expression. The messages conveyed through the words or look are potent parts of the punishment a child receives for misbehavior. They are reminders of what the child already knows, and their purpose is to vividly underscore that earlier lesson so that it can be put to the proper present use. Self-control is the result of continuous reminders that help turn learned responses into good habits. Often a child will repeat the parent's words for exactly that purpose, to reaffirm to him- or herself that a particular class of behavior is unacceptable.

Let's go back to little Ralph, who is tempted to throw another tantrum a week after the incident with the ice cream truck. This time, his mother is helping him to get dressed in the morning, and he insists he wants to wear his Farmer Brown bib overalls with the big jailhouse stripes instead of the more sedate denims his mother has laid out on his bed. Mommy explains that because the stripers no longer fit Ralph, she has passed them along to a neighbor boy who is six months younger. But the real problem, as usual, does not lie in rational facts; rather, it is in Ralph's realization that once again he is not getting his way. His lower lip begins to quiver ominously, much as the rim of a volcano will tremble before an eruption, and he takes a deep breath.

At precisely that moment, his mother leans down toward him with a patient smile and speaks the following words: "We do not scream and yell." The tantrum over the ice cream was not Ralph's first time-out, nor was it even the most

> Self-control is the result of continuous reminders that help turn learned responses into good habits.

recent; twice more in the intervening week, he had been placed back in the time-out chair with a firm "We do not . . . ." But today, for the first time, he pauses, and it is apparent that, at long last, he is weighing his options. The trembling of the lip subsides. As he lets out the breath he has collected for his customary aria, he repeats his mother's words: "We do not scream and yell just because we don't get our way." That repetition internalizes the lesson and gives him ownership of the decision to control his behavior.

Step Three: Self-Control

The third and final step in the process of learning self-control occurs when the internalization process is complete and the child is able to make that kind of decision about his behavior on his own. When that first happens, it is not uncommon for the "We do not . . ." phrase to be used again. But this time it is coming from little Ralph, who is fast becoming big Ralph.

15

Time-Outs:
The Specifics

❮❮◦——◦❯❯

THE GREAT BEHAVIORIST B. F. Skinner referred to positive reinforcement as largely a "silent" process, meaning that the results are seldom spectacular or seen immediately. Silence itself plays an important
role in raising children successfully, and there is no part of that journey in which this is more the case than in time-outs. The primary and
principal reason time-outs fail is that the parents, not the child, have
not yet learned to keep quiet.

Children who engage in destructive behavior such as biting, hitting,
kicking, and throwing tantrums are often given rational, reasonable
explanations for why those behaviors are unacceptable This can work
up to a point, but the more often a child gets that parental response,
the more likely it is that the words are falling on deaf ears. Words and
other stimuli are usually ineffective unless at some time they have been
linked to meaningful consequences. Reinforcement encourages behav-

ior, and punishment deters it. The situation will only deteriorate further until the children are punished.

Time-Out Means Time-Out from Reinforcement

An analog of this situation in adult behavior is when a speeder is stopped on the highway, only to be lectured briefly by the policeman and let go with just a warning. In many cases, the lecture works, but for habitual speeders, their reasoning is that if it didn't cost anything the last time, why not keep on doing it? A related example that comes to mind is the case of a medical student I once met at a lecture who told me he had saved hundreds of dollars a year by not paying the toll in his daily commute on the Massachusetts Turnpike. Whenever he waved an empty hand over the change basket and then drove on, the only consequence he discovered was that a buzzer went off. He told me he wasn't one of Pavlov's dogs and wasn't going to let a buzzer control his behavior. (A word to the wise: This story is decades old, before tollbooths could capture license plate numbers on surveillance cameras and computers issued expensive tickets.)

> Words and other stimuli are usually ineffective unless at some time they have been linked to meaningful consequences.

Children need more than the buzz of hollow words to help them learn to control serious misbehavior. The same logic applies to parents who keep up a stream of dialogue with a child during time-out or who send the offender into a roomful of diversions in the hope of teaching a lesson. In order for a three- to five-minute time-out to be effective, it must be time-out from all competing stimuli that could be viewed as a reward for misbehavior. This means:

> Children need more than the buzz of hollow words to help them learn to control serious misbehavior.

1. Nothing to look at
2. Nothing to do
3. No one to talk with
4. Nothing to listen to

The experience must be as close to a total absence of reinforcing consequences as is humanly—and humanely—possible. Time-out is to be used only in the home, only in the presence of the immediate family, and only for the following out-of-control behaviors:

1. Tantrums
2. Hitting
3. Biting
4. Throwing
5. Writing on walls
6. Destructiveness

Time Is of the Essence

Time-out must never be applied in arrears, significantly after the misbehavior in question has ended. It should be used *only* by a parent and *only* at the time when the serious, destructive, or dangerous behavior has been directly observed. Here's how it works, step-by-step, using a son as an example.

1. Take the child firmly by the hand and tell him, "We do not have tantrums (or whatever)." You *must* use the construction "We do not . . . ."
2. Seat him quickly in a small chair facing a blank wall.
3. At all times remain within one or two feet of the seated child.
4. If he attempts to leave the chair, *without saying a word* gently return him to the chair with your hands.
5. *Above all, avoid a chase.* A chase is fun. Time-out is not fun.
6. If he yells, screams, kicks the wall, curses, or says he has to go to the bathroom, *ignore him.* Do not say a single word.
7. He must remain in the chair a minimum of three minutes.
8. Do not set a timer; use a watch that he cannot see.
9. Do not say how long it will be—for all the child knows, it could be 300 minutes.
10. Do not say, "Be quiet" or "Sit still." Say nothing.
11. If the child tries to reason with you, to chat, or to ask questions, *do not respond—not a word.*
12. If he is still acting up after three minutes, wait until he stops and has been seated quietly for at least five seconds. If he continues to carry on for four or as much as five minutes, wait until he has been quiet for just two or three seconds. Then quickly go to him and say, "You have been quite well behaved. You may now leave the chair." But never say that until he has been quiet for at least a few seconds.
13. If he refuses to leave the chair, tell him he can leave whenever he wants. Don't wait around for him to get up—just go about your normal business.

14. If he wants to talk about the incident afterward, the only thing you may say to him is, "We do not . . . "—naming the behavior that got him in trouble. As long as he stays on the subject, say it over and over again like a broken record.

Showing Trumps Telling

Changing behavior by changing consequences is much more powerful than trying to apply logic or reason. Every parent wants to help a child connect the dots in life, but showing is far more effective than merely telling. If explaining things to children eventually works, it's only after they reach a point where they want to please the parent—which is not a priority among children at the outset of this program.

A fundamental principle of the time-out is that it is a punishment and not a reward. It is intended to discourage negative behaviors. It is different from a spanking or yelling or intimidation, all of which are far more likely to reinforce negative behavior than to end it. Instead, it offers a stimulus-free setting in which negative behavior is interrupted or at least contained, an environment that is uncomfortable for a child seeking attention and the reward of interaction. Time-out supplies a static-free, interruption-free, distraction-free—and, most of all, reinforcement-free—setting in which children are able to recall and process the messages they otherwise keep missing. And that's the next step in turning those messages into learning that can change their lives.

16

THE NURTURE RESPONSE
AND THE POWER
OF PRAISE

❦ ⸺ ❦

SEVERAL DECADES AGO, when I was doing an internship at a VA
hospital in Brockton, Massachusetts, I attended a discharge conference
in which a psychiatrist was interviewing a patient who had been in government mental hospitals for seventeen years. A standard procedure for
such conferences is that staff members of the hospital who have had
any contact with the patient ask questions that will shed light on
whether he is ready to function outside of this sheltered environment.
Over the years, I've heard half a dozen jokes about what happens in
these evaluations, and the premise is always that the patient is so desperate to get out that he will say anything. That's not the reality, though:
most patients who still need the kind of help they can get only on the
inside are not eager to be cast adrift without it.

In this particular interview, the psychiatric patient answered every question as normally as you or I would. The psychiatrist asked the final question: "To what do you attribute the fact that after seventeen years you are about to be discharged?"

The answer was, on the surface, wonderful: "The Lord has given me the strength and spiritual stamina to make the necessary changes in how I see the world, and for that I am thankful."

The psychiatrist said to the group, "This man will not be discharged," slapping the table with finality.

Two weeks later I attended the next conference, when the same patient again appeared before the interview panel. He was asked all the same questions as before, and he gave substantially the same answers—balanced, thoughtful, and entirely rational. The answers were all the same, that is, except for the concluding one. When asked why he felt he was ready to be discharged, this time he responded, "It's because of the Thorazine." The medication, which he had been taking every day, was in fact responsible for his radically changed behavior.

The psychiatrist had told me after the first meeting that one of the greatest risks facing patients who have been hospitalized for a long time is that they become unreliable about taking their medication. This is partly because when they are outside, they have to do for themselves what until then had been done for them, but the biggest reason is that as they get used to feeling normal, there are no real reminders in an average day that they feel that way because of the medicine. This is a particularly insidious problem with bipolar patients, who tend to become manic if they allow such lapses, so the worse they get, the better they feel.

The story about the patient in the VA hospital has two happy endings. The first one is that after he acknowledged the central role of the medicine in the improvement of his mental health, it was clear from the expressions around the table that he had passed the final exam.

When he saw this response, he then felt it safe to add, "And I thank God for the Thorazine." This time, the psychiatrist smiled. The other happy ending, of course, is that he was discharged.

So, now you may be asking, what does that story have to do with bringing up a healthy child?

Well, it isn't about drugs. I do recognize that there are powerful new medicines for the relief of mental illness, and I do believe that in the right circumstances—a sine qua non of which is an accurate diagnosis—they should be prescribed and that the results can be wonderful. But I also believe that the notion that 20 percent of America's schoolchildren merit such a diagnosis and need this kind of mind-altering, mood-changing medication is just plain crazy.

Cause and Effect

Here's what the Thorazine story has to do with children. I meet with the parents of children who have behavioral problems every day. Often, after a few weeks, positive changes occur in their children's behavior. When I ask the parents to explain the source of these changes, often they will get it right: they have been following my typewritten recommendations, and they can measure the improvement in the child's self-esteem, empathy, and self-control. But sometimes they get it wrong, and their answers can be as far off-target as that of the patient at the VA hospital. I've had parents tell me the behavior improved because it was spring or because the child had a haircut. Others have credited a recent vacation, a heart-to-heart with the child's teacher, or a change in diet. One mother told me she thought it was because just after they started seeing me, they bought their daughter a kitten and now she's like a different person. If it were that easy, there would be a lot more families with cats.

In every case, the improvements begin with recognizing good behavior—empathy, patience, sibling caring, self-control—and rewarding it with systematic, thoughtful, carefully targeted praise. But by itself, praise for these behaviors is not enough.

Praise gives a child only five or ten seconds of positive interaction at the time of the event that elicits it. If you multiply that by the six to ten occasions during the week that are recorded in a typical diary, it amounts to only one minute, more or less, of reinforcement for the types of behavior that you hope will shape their lives. That's not enough. The positive behaviors have to be nurtured in other ways as well.

The Nurture Response

The nurture response takes place in the following steps. A half hour to eight to ten hours after the behavior, the parent takes the child aside in private and carefully reconstructs the favorable event in vivid detail. The child is told why the specific behavior is valued. The purpose is to allow the child to relive the event in his or her mind's eye. Then, as before, it is immediately followed by 100 percent praise. The parent labels this behavior as grown-up, big-boy or big-girl, mature. This is followed in turn by ten or fifteen minutes of special time.

Why did I say 100 percent praise? Because, as with every other kind of medicine, praise comes in a variety of forms, sizes, and strengths. The poet Alexander Pope

Parents need to put a lot more energy into complimenting a child than they would an adult, and they've got to be very specific about why the behavior is so laudable.

was deriding the application of an insignificant dose when he coined the expression to "damn with faint praise"—that is, to offer praise that is so weak that it does more harm than good. How many of us would waste time on a movie that someone has described with an indifferent shrug as "OK"? Or, imagine the letdown you'd experience after working all night to complete a project, only to have a superior reward the effort with a weak handshake or a perfunctory, "Nice job." Parents need to put a lot more energy into complimenting a child than they would an adult, and they've got to be very specific about why the behavior is so laudable.

Most of all, they can't weaken the medicine and undercut its intended purpose by sending a mixed message. You should not give the child half praise and half criticism.

Here are some examples of the kind of thing to avoid:

"Gee, Charlie, your mom and I are so proud you got that A in spelling—we couldn't believe it was our little boy!"

"Annie, you were such a big girl for sharing the peanuts with your brother Ben. See how much better you feel than when you keep them all to yourself?"

"You were so polite to Mrs. Nelson this afternoon. Why can't you be that way all the time?"

"You did such a good job making your bed this morning, and it took only a minute. Next time, try to remember how easy it is when you complain that you don't have the time."

"You showed a lot of self-control when your mommy said you couldn't have any ice cream just before bedtime. You keep acting that grown-up, and pretty soon you won't be fat anymore."

"You were certainly a good sport to congratulate Jack and Freddie for winning the three-legged race. I expected you to burst into tears."

Now for a couple of examples of the nurture response in which the parents get it right.

In the first case, Catherine, 3, can't find her piglet doll to take on a shopping trip with Mommy. After a reasonable search, she decides, "I'll take the duck instead." At the time of the decision, her mother tells her that she's a big girl and that she's proud of her. Three hours later, when Daddy is home from work, both parents vividly remind her of the incident. They tell her they knew she was very disappointed, they wished she could have found the piglet, and they were so proud of her for taking this disappointment in a calm manner like a real big girl. They spend the next ten or fifteen minutes talking about the shopping trip and the fun they have together, and Daddy tells her about something nice that happened at work that reminded him how lucky he is to have Catherine for a daughter.

In the second case, Amy, 6, helps search for a special pair of shoes that she outgrew two years before and had been set aside for her little sister to wear to kindergarten. The search is unsuccessful, and when the sister starts to cry, Amy consoles her and tells her that they'll look again that afternoon, when they both get back home, and that the sister can wear another pair that are "just as nice." The consolation stops the tears, but more important, it demonstrates sibling caring and a mature response to disappointment. That afternoon, when the children return, the mother takes Amy aside and vividly reminds her of what happened that morning. "I know how you loved those shoes when they were yours, and you were so good to help look for them. We saw how disappointed your sister was, and I know you were disappointed too. But you put all that aside so that you could make your sister feel better." She tells her how proud she was of her and what a big girl she is, how grown-up, and then spends ten more minutes talking with her about what happened that day in school.

When parents learn to nurture positive behavior in this way—(A) citing the specific incident in vivid detail, (B) giving the child 100 percent praise, (C) immediately explaining why the behavior is of value (because it means the child is being grown-up), and (D) sharing several minutes of special time—just six times a week, the child will be receiving at least an hour a week of parenting attention and praise for the behaviors they want to encourage. This increased attention is now enough to effectively compete with all the attention that the child has been receiving for behavior that is negative. Parents find the four-step nurture response, as just outlined, easy to remember and turn into a habit: we call it the ABCD sequence.

Learning What Is Praiseworthy

Even before initiating this technique, parents will report that their children are already starting to behave in far more positive ways simply because the desired behaviors are being praised and being described as those of a mature, grown-up big boy or big girl. But after the start of the nurture response, which is typically around the beginning of the third week, the improvement accelerates appreciably. It is not uncommon for parents to say that they feel they have traded their former children, who were so difficult, for new ones who are delightful.

On the other hand, I occasionally am asked whether it's possible to praise too much, and sometimes parents are surprised when I answer yes. As a rule people praise their children naturally and hardly think about it. We know that praise is good, and for most parents it's easy. We also know that parental praise builds self-esteem, the quiet inner feeling of competence that helps determine success in life.

But what happens when the praise is frequent, lavish, and nearly automatic, regardless how worthy the cause? For one thing, when parents praise practically everything, it can discourage development of the child's ability to internalize positive consequences, to know without being told by others that he or she is doing well. For another, too much of anything can encourage overdependence, even external words of approval.

Early on, every child needs words of praise, sincere approval, and nurture for ordinary behaviors. It isn't long before that need reduces, however, and we must attempt to prepare the child for a world in which praise is not given repeatedly for everything that may deserve it. Besides, when a child is told for the first time that he or she is admirable for helping mother, coping with disappointment, or caring for a friend, the impact of that praise is bound to be different from when the same affirmation is offered for the hundredth time for precisely the same things. Most children will interpret too frequent parental praise as insincere, or even manipulative, as they begin to realize that pats on the back don't occur that often elsewhere.

Conversely, I have met parents who feel that praise isn't good for a child, or that it is something meant for only very young children. They feel that a child should behave well without encouragement—a reasonable long-term goal but a disastrous starting point. Often it's difficult for such parents to praise, even when it is explained to them how praise and the teachable moment work. When they suggest that "virtue is its own reward," they deprive their child of the fundamental nurture by which virtue or anything else we consider "praiseworthy" is learned.

Good or bad behaviors do not spring unbidden from hidden reservoirs within the mind. The determining factor in how your child acts is not some inner demon or angel. It is learning, plain and simple. And the way learning happens is through encouragement n the form of time and attention for particular kinds of behavior. Children need to have someone be proud of them before they can develop feelings of self-worth. It's no virtue to behave well in your young years if the behavior is little more than a happy accident and you really don't know what virtue is all about. The true "reward" for virtue happens when reinforcing words of external praise gradually become internalized in a character pattern of cause and effect—"I am a worthwhile person."

Learning to Praise

But what about the parent who doesn't know how to praise? One mother told me that even when her son did something well, her praise sounded false to them both. "Maybe it has to do with my own childhood," she said. "I was never praised."

That same mother later admitted to me that she had never really thought much of herself, and that recognition gave her the insight to how important it was that she learn to praise her son. He had been having trouble getting along with other children, and her goal was to encourage new winning-friends behaviors.

"It works," she told me a few weeks later. "He's a changed boy." She thought for a moment and added, "It works for me, too. It's not so hard for me to see the good things he does and to say how much I like to see him behaving that way. I even find myself

> The true "reward" for virtue happens when reinforcing words of external praise gradually become internalized in a character pattern of cause and effect—"I am a worthwhile person."

doing it with his two sisters, who don't have behavior problems. They really look pleased when I give them a little pat on the back."

Another common belief among parents is that praise simply isn't good for a child, that it will lead to bad behavior, and that a more reliable route to good behavior is criticism. Sometimes this is because the parents believe that anything good has to be paid for, that there's no pleasure without pain. But they are wrong in thinking that withholding praise has no effect. A child who is not praised has no guidelines for what the parents think is valuable. Praising *specific behaviors* will never lead to bad behavior. Nonspecific praise ("You are a good boy/girl.") may result in bad behavior because no child will ever feel 100 percent good. As for the notion that criticism is a better teacher than praise, consider what is being taught. If unconditional praise so provably builds self-esteem, then the opposite of praise, which is criticism, will likely tear it down.

17

THE ABCDS OF CHANGED BEHAVIOR

❦──❖

AS I SAID, the nurture response described in the previous chapter, which is in four steps, is referred to as the ABCD sequence. For easy reference, here those steps are again:

A. Take the child aside in private. Vividly remind him or her of the behavior noted in the diary. Using words makes the behavior come to life again in his or her mind's eye. For example: "When I told you we were going for a walk, you sat down on the bottom step of the front-hall stairs and let me help you put on your pretty, red-rubber boots."

B. Immediately follow that with 100 percent praise. "I'm so proud of you!" Praise that is mixed with criticism—"I'm glad you didn't throw a tantrum the way you did yesterday"—should be avoided like poison, because that's what it is.

C. Then immediately put into words why this behavior is valued and what it means to you. "That was very *grown-up*. You're such a big boy/big girl. When you're helpful like that, it reminds me of how big you are." (*Don't* undercut this praise by saying "good boy/good girl" or "good job.")

D. Follow this immediately with five or ten minutes of doing something you know the child enjoys. It could be just sitting and talking, singing together, playing with a pet, taking turns combing each other's hair, or tossing a ball back and forth. In this step, children don't need to be told that you're taking this special time because they sat still while you helped them put on their boots. In fact, it's far better to let them make the association themselves—which they inevitably will.

Marshmallow Moments

This is a good place for the marshmallow story. It's about children, but it has a powerful message for parents.

Several years ago, a behavioral psychologist ran an experiment on delayed gratification and how children learn patience. The study was conducted in a small Midwestern town, and its subjects were first graders—perhaps twenty of them—who were in their first week of school. The children were taken one at a time into a room, where they were introduced to the psychologist and asked some standard questions such as name, age, and address. Then, at the same point in each interview, the psychologist would suddenly look at his watch as though recalling a prior appointment and tell the child that he had to leave for a little while. He would ask if the child minded. No child ever did, but the psychologist would nevertheless make a show of figuring out how to atone for the inconvenience. After a moment's thought, he would ask if the child liked marshmallows. The answer was always yes. The psychologist would then open his briefcase, produce a marshmallow, and offer the child a choice. He or she could eat the marshmallow right away, and that would be just fine. Or the child could wait until the psychologist returned, and if the first marshmallow was still there, he would give the child a second one as a reward for exhibiting patience and restraint.

Naturally, a certain number of children responded to the offer by grabbing at the prize and popping it into their mouths before the psychologist left the room. A slightly smaller number left the marshmallow just where it was on the table and didn't even look at it until the psychologist came back, typically in about three minutes. There was a third group, however, for whom the choice comprised an epic struggle. As the psychologist watched through a mirrored window, each of these children battled visibly with the temptation. Some put forth a hand and then pulled it back, others forced themselves to look elsewhere to avoid thinking about it, and some even got out of the chair and with strained resolve walked around the marshmallow to the far side of the room. Of that third group, more eventually succumbed to the lure of gratification than successfully waited for the delayed reward.

I don't know what the study proved, but the real payoff on the experiment came twelve years later. The psychologist realized that the children he had tested as first graders were about to graduate from high school, and when he checked on the names in the senior class, he saw that almost all of the original kids were still in the same school system. His follow-up to the original study produced some fascinating results.

The children who had shown the most self-control at the start of their education were showing that same ability—and reaping its rewards—when they reached commencement. They had better academic records, led more successful social lives, and were more decisive.

Every one of the kids who had been willing to wait for the reward at the age of 6 had made plans for his or her long-term future, principally in regard to continuing education, in which the rewards, like that second marshmallow, were just over the horizon and beyond their present view. And if you want some hard numbers, the kids who got the second marshmallow scored an average of 210 points higher on their SATs—getting 610 on verbal and 652 on quantitative—than the average for the kids who didn't wait.

The Power of Example

The ability to manage our impulses is not an instinct or a genetic gift—although it is often a legacy from our parents, which they have passed along to us by example. First and foremost, it is a matter of deliberate and habitual choice. Many parents tell me sad stories of how they were physically punished as children and say they have determined not to repeat that mistake in responding to challenges from their own kids. But if the impulse is there, I urge you to consider the parable of the second marshmallow. Instead of counting to ten before chasing the child from the room, try the far more effective ABCD sequence.

The simple ABCD nurture response produces three positive results, even if they don't happen all at once and the ultimate benefits accumulate beyond our immediate horizon:

First, it increases the frequency of the desired behav-

> The ability to manage our impulses is not an instinct or a genetic gift—although it is often a legacy from our parents, which they have passed along to us by example.

ior by the child—a corollary to which, of course, is that it reduces the frequency of the kind of behavior that drives parents crazy.

Second, it increases self-esteem. This happens as the reinforcing words and actions are internalized and eventually replace punishment and criticism as the standard for how children feel about themselves.

And third, by the power of example and by the natural urge to reciprocity, it increases the feelings of warmth and caring by the child toward the parents. Hillel's quote from Chapter

> Instead of counting to ten before chasing the child from the room, try the far more effective ABCD sequence.

11 echoes here: "If you come to my house," your child will tell you by words and actions, "I will come to yours."

18

THIRTY DAYS THAT
LAST A LIFETIME

❧———❧

THIS THIRTY-DAY PROGRAM works because the parent becomes the teacher. And of course, the new behaviors last much more than thirty days—they last as long as the parent continues in that role, teaching behaviors that the child needs to learn in order to live in the real world. Like all learned behaviors, they continue long after the teacher is no longer there.

Improvement Doesn't Equal Cure

There's a hitch, however. The very fact that the program can produce such fast results sometimes creates a problem. Beware of confusing early signs of improvement in a child's behavior with long-term benefit. Although I always caution parents in advance that this approach is not a quick fix, I frequently hear after three or four visits that the problems have been solved. I know they haven't. One swallow maketh not a summer.

A friend of mine recently returned from South Africa, where he had participated in a medical mission to a rural village ravaged by AIDS. It was his third such visit, and he was gratified to see some of the changes that had taken place as results of his earlier trips. But one development was very disturbing. In many cases, when patients had started getting better after taking the medicine he prescribed, they stopped the treatment. One reason was that after improving to a level where they felt comfortable, they began giving their medicine to someone else in their family or in the village who also suffered from AIDS and had not been treated. An outsider may view this sharing as a laudable form of altruism, but in fact it was a fatal mistake. These patients misread the early improvement as a sign that they'd been healed, and when they stopped the medicine, their disease resumed its inevitable course—and they died. Moreover, the other AIDS sufferers to whom they'd given their medication now could no longer get the treatment, since their source was gone, and they died as well.

> **B**eware of confusing early signs of improvement in a child's behavior with long-term benefit.

This story isn't offered as a report of some faraway village; it's about human nature. The same thing happens in this country every day, although usually with less tragic consequences. One of the most common risks for Americans who are prescribed antibiotics is that they stop taking them as soon as they start feeling better, and because they don't complete the course of treatment, the disease returns with a vengeance. Likewise, early signs of improvement in your child's behavior should not be taken as the occasion for a premature "Mission Accomplished" party. Instead, they should become incentives to continue systematic reinforcement of that behavior by the same techniques that encouraged it in the first place.

The behaviors that this program teaches develop fundamental social skills—expressing concern about the needs, feelings, and wishes of others; caring for siblings; and taking disappointment calmly. We live in a world where disappointment will always be a part of living, and a calm response is another indication of mature behavior and self-control.

Guiding Lights

Benjamin Spock might have been right when he said that children can find their way to adulthood simply by following their own will. But today we are surrounded with evidence of what adulthood holds for those who are forced to make the journey without responsible and loving guidance. Every child must be helped to make the transition from the natural self-centeredness of infancy to the interconnectedness and mutuality of responsible maturity. Children need parental help in transiting from the fears and frustrations that are concomitant with the relative powerlessness of childhood.

The journey from out-of-control to self-control is never successfully completed alone. Socialization is

> Every child must be helped to make the transition from the natural self-centeredness of infancy to the interconnectedness and mutuality of responsible maturity.

a learned skill, and learning requires teachers. It is the natural job of parents to show children how to become civilized, social human beings who know how to relate to disappointment and to others around them with care, self-control, and sensitivity. It is not the parents' job to protect their children from the disappointments, hurts, and losses of a normal childhood. Instead, they must help their children learn from those experiences—to extract the gold from the refiner's fire.

I mentioned in Chapter 3 that growing up resembles the process by which our bodies develop the natural defense of a healthy immune system. We don't gain that protection by living in isolation. That's why mothers sometimes have chicken-pox or measles parties—the body learns to live through these infectious assaults and recover from them before the children reach an age where those diseases are likely to do significantly greater damage. In the same way, children who are exposed to life's challenges early, in a safely managed environment, are far better equipped to deal with those same risks when they face them alone as teens or adults. How can children learn to take disappointment calmly when their parents make sure that they are seldom disappointed? How can they develop empathy unless they have lived through hurts of their own? And how can they learn to survive if their overly protective parents, metaphorically and sometimes literally, seldom let them out of the house?

19

"JUST SAY NO" TO DRUGGING YOUR CHILD

<figure>※ ○──── ○ ※</figure>

FOR MOST CHILDREN, the first prolonged out-of-the-house experience comes with the start of formal schooling. Parents normally regard this event as a kind of double commencement. Foremost, it is a launchpad for the child into the greater world beyond the home. Also, by shifting a part of their responsibility as parents to other caring hands, in many cases it restores a degree of the freedom that the mother and father had given up to childbirth five years or more before.

But how safe is that transition for the child? How likely are the owners of those other hands to put the child's interests ahead of their own? Is the parents' freedom sometimes purchased at a hidden cost to the child that can have disastrous long-term consequences? And if so, does this potentially ruinous process begin only with the start of school? These are questions all parents think about, but most never ask. Instead, they assume the issues they represent are covered by the constitution or the law and somehow woven into our contract as members of a civilized society.

They should be, but they're not.

Voices in the Wilderness

In February 2000, Dr. Joseph T. Coyle, chairman of the department of psychiatry at Harvard Medical School, wrote an editorial in the *Journal of the American Medical Association* about the drugging of kids with behavioral problems. Describing the practice as subjecting children to "quick and inexpensive pharmacologic fixes," he said there was "no empirical evidence to support psychotropic drug use in very young children."

The following month, less than a year before the end of the Clinton presidency, the *New York Times* reported that the White House was launching "a major effort to reverse a sharp increase in the number of preschool children using Ritalin, Prozac and other powerful psychiatric drugs." The effort was four-pronged: educating parents about the risks in using these drugs, mandating new drug labels, studying the use of Ritalin in children under the age of 6, and holding a conference on diagnosing and treating mental illness in very young children.

Dr. Steven E. Hyman, head of the National Institute of Mental Health, told the *Times*, "As a rule of thumb, doctors, psychologists and social workers should attempt to modify the behavior of a child and deal with family crises before drugs are prescribed." Hyman wasn't against the use of drugs across the board; he reserved them for "otherwise uncontrollable" behaviors such as aggression, self-mutilation, or head banging. But he said children were being medicated without the proper evaluation and without any attempt at behavior modification.

Despite this hopeful attempt to reverse the tide of childhood drugging, the administration changed a few months later, and today the flow of psychopharmaceuticals into the brains and bodies of America's children is at an all-time high and continuing to rise. In addition to the millions of children who have been locked into a regimen of daily drugging for the phantom diagnosis of ADHD, millions more are prescribed potent, habit-forming antidepressants that have been linked to a diagnosis that is far more tangible—childhood suicide. For a more detailed discussion of how the psychiatric establishment has hijacked America's school systems, read *Child Drugging—Psychiatry Destroying Lives: Report and Recommendations of Fraudulent Psychiatric Diagnosis and the Enforced Drugging of Youth*, published by the Citizens Commission on Human Rights, a California-based parents' advocacy group.

Fatal Flaws

Another CCHR publication, *The Silent Death of America's Children*, based on a presentation to the President's New Freedom Commission on Mental Health in 2002, offers some shocking case histories of psychiatric abuses of children:

- A California boy of 14, diagnosed with ADHD, was prescribed a powerful stimulant. His parents were told that if they objected, they could be charged for "neglecting his educational and emotional needs." He died of a heart attack from the stimulant.
- A Pennsylvania girl of 10, whose chief offense was "talking out of turn" in school, was given the same diagnosis after a thirty-minute meeting with a psychiatrist—without any tests or physical examination. She then was prescribed three different psychiatric drugs in succession, and she died of convulsions.

• On a physician referral from her school, a first grader in Ohio was put on a stimulant to help her "stay on task." After five years of stomach pains, nausea, mood swings, and bizarre behavior, which her parents associated with the drug, she died in her sleep from cardiac arrhythmia.

• Another Ohio child, a boy of 13, appeared to be having some trouble adjusting to a new neighborhood and school system, so teachers told the parents they should seek "professional help." They found a psychiatrist who gave the boy a free sample of an antidepressant with no printed information on risks or side effects. If he wasn't clinically depressed before the drug, he was afterward; a week after he started taking it, he committed suicide.

• Two days after he began withdrawal from stimulants prescribed for hyperactivity, another boy committed suicide the same way, by hanging, at the age of 10.

The same publication reports on studies showing that up to 83 percent of people referred to psychiatrists actually suffered from an undiagnosed physical illness, including 42 percent who had been diagnosed with psychoses. Often the real problem was nothing more complicated than diet. A shift away from fats and sugars to fruits, vegetables, and whole grains reduced "antisocial behavior" by 47 percent in one California study in juvenile institutions, and it increased the academic performance of children in California schools by 16 percent. In the study with the schools, the so-called learning disabilities—many of which are the diagnostic basis for drugging—declined by a dramatic 40 percent.

Taking a Stand

What can parents do in response to the challenge of a diagnosis for their child of a condition such as ADHD? If you are one of the people who have a hard time understanding why some kids don't always "just say no" to recreational drugs, as Nancy Reagan suggested they should, then you might be surprised at how hard the system can make it for you when you try to say the same thing on behalf of your own child. It isn't a matter of just withholding permission as one might for a field trip, or of deciding what your child will have for lunch. Parents who decline permission to have their children medicated for behavior problems often are confronted by the combined authority of the school system and the medical profession and threatened with legal reprisals including expulsion, court proceedings, and even the potential loss of custody of their children.

As the first step in coping with this threat, the CCHR recommends that parents should take the time to educate themselves. This means learning everything they need to know to ensure that the information they are given by the family doctor, by the schools' teachers, nurses, and psychologists, and by any consulting psychiatrists is accurate and complete and that it is presented in a useful way, without bias or the intent to sell a benefit to the school at the expense of the child. With as many as 20 percent of the children in some school districts on some form of prescription psychotropic medication, it's a safe bet that the huge majority of their parents did not do this and that they have no idea of the risks or of their options.

A shift away from fats and sugars to fruits, vegetables, and whole grains reduced "antisocial behavior" by 47 percent in one California study in juvenile institutions, and it increased the academic performance of children in California schools by 16 percent.

The CCHR also advises parents to let the school know they will not give permission for the child to fill out any psychological test or questionnaire in the classroom. The results of such exercises are used as the basis for "diagnostic" screening and can lead to a prescription that the school or a psychiatrist may try forcing the child to take. Parents of children who have already started taking such medication are strongly warned to *not* terminate the treatment abruptly or without the supervision of a physician. With several such drugs, sudden withdrawal can lead to serious physical or psychological damage, including a higher risk of suicide.

If the school disregards your instructions or uses threats or coercion to force your child into the prescription program, consult with an attorney.

PART TWO

CASES

20

TERRIBLE EXAMPLES, TERRIFIC RESULTS

⟪∘———∘⟫

A NOTORIOUS GANGSTER escaped from custody, so the story goes, and was thought to be headed for his hometown in rural Georgia. The FBI collected mug shots from all of his earlier arrests—a total of eight—and mailed them to the local sheriff along with a copy of the current wanted poster. A few days later, the agent in charge called to see if the package had arrived. "Holy smoke! I'm way ahead of you," the sheriff replied. "We've seen all nine of them fellers. I've already got four of them in the lockup; we shot three more; and we're still out chasing the other two."

Nine Lives

The case histories featured in the following chapters have been organized on the basis of the parents' primary complaint about their chil-

T he first place any of us learns about child care is within our own families.

dren's behaviors. They do not appear in any sort of priority, so please don't infer that some complaints are worse or better than others. In fact, regardless of the chapter titles, there are elements of most of these behaviors in each of the case histories, whatever the primary complaint may be. Most likely, one or two of the chapter labels initially will pop out as a description of the particular behavior that is currently driving you crazy. But after reading further, you're probably going to respond much the way that the sheriff in Georgia did. "Holy smoke! We've seen all nine of them, and they're all upstairs right this minute, in our child's bedroom."

For that reason, I suggest that you read all nine case histories with equal care, even those that don't seem to apply to your child at first glance. After the first one, I've greatly abridged the details of my recommendations—which are obviously repetitious—in order to help keep us both awake. I start with tantrums because it's a complaint I hear frequently—but also because in this particular case history the mother supplied me with an unusual amount of detail, especially about the dialogue with her daughter.

There is also an unavoidable sameness to the ways in which most of the parents have responded to these challenges, usually based on bad advice from one or more of the hundreds of post-Freudian bestsellers on feel-good parenting. In every such case, that advice serves only to encourage the very behaviors it ostensibly aims to reverse. I have avoided redundancy in those parts of the stories by choosing examples in which the bad advice is specific to the class of behavior in focus. Each example is from a different source.

Why do I mention the advice that parents have received before they come to see me? The reason is that this advice is a huge part of the problem. Nobody seeks the services of a therapist before having tried elsewhere to gather information on the areas in which help is needed. The first place any of us learns about child care is within our own families. We also are exposed to uncountable numbers of magazine and newspaper articles, and there are enough books on the subject to fill a library.

Conventional Wisdom

When Dr. Barry Marshall discovered that the cause of stomach ulcers was the bacterium *h. pylori*, he was asked at a convention of skeptical gastroenterologists to estimate the percentage of such ulcers that he thought were due to that infectious cause. His answer, 100 percent, was so shockingly at odds with the conventional wisdom, which blamed stomach ulcers on stress, lifestyles, and diet, that he became an instant pariah. In my own field of psychology, behaviorists have been at war with Freudians for the better part of a century, which is long enough to build up a certain degree of immunity to institutional reprisals. Likewise, I doubtless am immune to a Nobel Prize, which was Marshall's well-deserved reward when the pendulum finally swung the other way.

But there is one thing that Dr. Marshall and I do have in common: our answers to the role of infection in the conditions we treat. In the case of parenting, the infection is not a bacterium but a widespread, fundamentally flawed concept: that any type of inappropriate childhood behavior—tantrums, lying, biting, spitting, drawing on the wallpaper, or threatening to punch one's mother—can be changed by the kinds of attention that simply encourage more of the same. Therefore, the following cases histories all begin, after the initial facts, with a reference to something the parents have read in a popular magazine or book—because that's how they start in real life. If any behaviorist is asked to estimate the number of parents whose view of the child-raising process is colored by this bad advice, the answer will be 100 percent.

Now open your mind wide and say, "Ah-h-h."

This won't hurt a bit.

21

TANTRUMS

‹‹•——•››

CHRISTIE STARTED HAVING tantrums at the age of 2, and by the time her parents came to see me, she was 5 years old. The tantrums were the first thing they told me about her—she had a lot of them. They added that she was demanding, didn't get along with her sister, and had an "intense" personality.

I asked for examples of the occasions when these tantrums took place and got an earful. The other day Christie had erupted because her mother had given her a muffin with peanut butter instead of dairy butter. Last night she was in the tub with her sister Suzanne, who is not quite 2, and she blew up—splashing water, yelling, and telling Suzanne she hated her—because she wanted "to be alone." She frequently decided she didn't want to get dressed in time for preschool, and one morning that week, she kept the tantrum going long enough to miss her ride.

When this pattern began three years ago, the parents ascribed it to the "Terrible Twos." Now that explanation no longer fit. How unusual was it, they asked, for a child to act that way? Was it still just a phase, and if so, how should they cope with it, and how much longer could they expect it to continue?

The mother also told me that Christie's relationship with her sister was driving her crazy. Christie wanted to tell Suzanne what to do—and what not to do—from dawn to dusk. They both had been given battery-operated

> When this pattern began three years ago, the parents ascribed it to the "Terrible Twos." Now that explanation no longer fit.

light wands by their grandmother, and whenever they played with them, if Suzanne's wand was off, Christie would scream at her until she turned it on. If it was on, she'd use the same tactic to make her turn it off. She was abusive and belittling and quickly resorted to force to get what she couldn't win by persuasion. Although the way she dealt with her sister in these conflicts was identical to the pattern she used with her parents, the mother saw it as a separate set of behaviors—which she described to me as sibling rivalry.

Nothing Works

Obviously, no parents reach for the yellow pages and call the nearest therapist the first time their daughter throws a fit. But after the first couple of explosions three years before, when it appeared the behavior might be settling into a disturbing pattern, Christie's parents turned to one of the familiar primers on child care. The first one they took from the shelf (written by the same reliable savant who had guided them successfully through both children's colic, Christie's measles, and a couple of sieges of croup) had become a virtual family bible. They followed its advice religiously for nearly a year, but apparently they were going about it in the wrong way, because Christie's behavior only worsened. They tried other advice books, initially from the local bookstore and then, when that became too expensive, from the library. Nothing worked. As the frequency of the tantrums increased, they began to lose their faith in the reigning gurus of child care.

The first time they visited my office, they brought along a list of the varied and fanciful explanations these books offered for their daughter's behavior. Christie, they read, was flooded with more emotions than her little mind could handle, and it was up to the parents to discover the particular cause of her behavior. Maybe she had been sitting too long. Perhaps she was overstimulated. Could she be saddened by some family crisis, such as the loss of a treasured pet?

Not one single book ever suggested that the reason for Christie's behavior might be simply that she was not getting her way.

Whether or not the diligent parents ever discovered the hidden cause, the books advised a variety of ways to end a tantrum and soothe the troubled child. Touch her and reassure her verbally. Hold her tight. Tell her, one book suggested, "It's all right to lose control." Another proposed a rhythmic, gentle stroking of the child's eyebrows. Regardless of how imaginative or diverse these nostrums may appear, they all had a common core: reinforcement of the behavior they were meant to end.

Christie's parents will probably never really know what precipitated the first tantrum, and I tried to reassure them that it didn't make the slightest difference. Even if that first agent is a mystery, an important and perhaps primary motive of the tantrums that followed should be as clear as glass. When the reward for uncontrolled behavior is hugs, reassurances, and eyebrow stroking, it's easy enough to figure out why it keeps repeating.

Setting Agendas

At the end of that introductory session, the parents and I wrote down some specific goals they hoped to achieve through our consultation:

1. Get Christie to start listening.
2. Eliminate the anger in the house.
3. Change the dominant mood from rage or the expectation of rage to one in which everyone is happy.
4. Teach the girls to get along with each other.

Most of the anger in the house was the result of the tantrums or the sibling rivalry. As a first step toward helping Christie, I gave them a more helpful list than the one they had brought with them. In the following week, the parents were to do three things:

1. Look for examples of *sibling caring*—the opposite of rivalry—instances in which Christie relates to her sister in a friendly, thoughtful way; *note these instances in a diary, and be specific.*
2. Look for and note any behaviors that indicate she is thinking of others, both within the family and beyond—*Mother Teresa behaviors.*
3. Since Christie's tantrums are the result of things not going her way, look for and note specific examples of the opposite, when she reacts reasonably even if she doesn't get what she wants—*taking disappointment calmly.*

The parents agreed to record four to six examples of these behaviors weekly—ideally, a couple from each category—in the diary notebook. This is the first step in the process of teaching Christie that these are valued behaviors and that her parents and her little sister all come closer together with her as a family when she treats them in these ways. I then guided them through the remaining steps in the process.

Things Are Really Looking Up

The following week, Christie's parents returned to my office, and we went through the items they had recorded in the diary. One of the examples of sibling-caring behavior that the mother had noted occurred during a hectic mealtime the previous noon. She had already given Christie her sandwich and a cup of soup, but just as she was putting a similar lunch in front of Suzanne, the doorbell and the telephone both rang at the same time. The mother had to sign for a package from UPS while negotiating a changed appointment with the children's pediatrician; meanwhile, the neglected younger child began to whimper. Christie put aside her sandwich, got up from her chair to find a clean spoon, and then carefully used it to feed the soup to her little sister. She used the same language—"Open wide," and "Down the little red lane"—that their mother had used with them both when they were much smaller. As the harried mother watched this interchange from across the room, she made a mental note to herself to enter it in the diary. She also realized that it was one of those perfect moments—a pure, unexpected gift that would last in her memory for years to come.

Two hours later, when Suzanne was down for her afternoon nap, the mother took Christie out on the porch and sat with her on the swing chair looking out over the flower and vegetable garden she had planted beside the garage. About once a week during the warm months, they would sit in this same place at dusk for a session of what Christie referred to as "pink cloud," watching the changing colors in the sky just after sunset. But this was the first time the mother could recall that she and her daughter had sat there together in the middle of the afternoon. She put her arm around Christie's shoulder and kissed her hair. "Do you remember feeding Suzanne her soup while I was at the door with the delivery man this noontime?" she asked.

Christie looked up at her speculatively and said yes. It was clear she recognized the approval in the tone of her mother's voice, but she wasn't certain where this was headed.

"You fed her before you fed yourself," the mother went on. "I saw you put your own sandwich back on the plate, and you jumped up to find a clean spoon for your little sister."

"She was hungry," Christie said. She was clearly glad her mother was recalling the event with such affection. "She was starting to cry."

"That's right, she was starting to cry. And she stopped when you began feeding her. You are such a loving sister, and such a help to your mother. That was a very *grown-up* thing to do. I am so proud of you, Christie."

The mother looked down and saw her daughter taking it in. After a moment, Christie raised her eyes to the sky above the garage roof, and her mother suddenly was certain she knew exactly what she was thinking. "Being together like this on the swing chair is like pink cloud, isn't it?"

Thoughtfully, Christie shook her head. "No," she said after a moment's reflection. "It's better."

They spent the next ten minutes discussing Christie's plans to learn to talk to cats and dogs and to become an animal trainer or a veterinarian.

The tantrums tapered off, and a few months later they came to an end. As of this writing, Christie is 16 and earns honors grade as a popular junior in high school. Her career plans have shifted; she does extremely well in science and is now thinking of becoming an anthropologist. As far as I know, she never did learn to talk to animals. Her little sister is in middle school. Christie told their mother she considers Suzanne to be one of her best friends.

22

DESTRUCTIVE BEHAVIOR

❦ ❖ ❦

TOMMY IS 3, and if he doesn't get what he wants, when he wants it, he can make Tony Soprano seem like a pretty reasonable guy. When he decides he's thirsty, for example, he often doesn't even wait for his father to put down whatever he may be holding before he starts to scream and throw things. At one time or another—and in some of the following examples, more than one time—he has squirted liquid dishwasher soap onto the walls and draperies, covered his face and hair with his mother's lipstick, written on the walls with such force that the pencil tore the paper, poured coffee onto his parents' bed, run screaming into the street, and sprinkled a whole jar of minced onions, juice and all, onto the living-room oriental rug. "I begged him not to spill the onions," his mother said. "He grabbed the jar from the kitchen counter, and I pleaded with him to give it back. He just smiled as though he thought it was all a big joke. The more I begged, the bigger the smile got."

"There's a word for that," the father offered, rolling his eyes toward my office ceiling.

"What's that?" I asked.

He shifted his weight in the chair. "Sadism?" He laughed uncomfortably and then added, "That isn't what I really think. I guess I'm trying to make a joke of it."

"We *are* worried sick about Tommy," the mother cut in, "but I also think we're giving you the wrong impression. Most of what he does is perfectly—well—perfectly normal."

I asked her to tell me about some of those normal things, and she ticked off a few highlights before faltering. He learned to walk at the age of 8 months. He took pride in the fact that he could dress himself, and although there were frequent spills, he was also getting pretty good at pouring his milk. He knew how to use the toilet, and he loved to flush. "But then yesterday he stood on a stool at the kitchen cleaning cabinet," she said with a note of distress, "which I've repeatedly told him not to do, and he brought down a bottle of Lysol on his head, soaking himself from top to bottom."

"He's gotten famous in the neighborhood," the father volunteered. "Everybody knows him, and they all love him. He's a cute, funny, exuberant little guy. But I don't think we have a neighbor within five houses on either side of us who hasn't brought him back home at one time or another after he's run out when he shouldn't have."

"—usually without a stitch of clothes on," his wife pointed out with a woebegone smile. "It's one of his favorite things."

They told me some more of the things Tommy was good at. He knew how to call his grandmother, whose number was at the top of the speed-dial listing on the telephone, which they all thought was remarkable. Because he had heard the stories so often, he was able to "read" whole sentences from the familiar children's books that his parents shared with him at bedtime. He had a wry and impish sense of humor and loved to play tickle games and hide-and-seek. He took delight in singing along with the Muppets on "Sesame Street." He got along famously with his brother, Michael, who was 8, and was amazingly agile, for his age, in trying to keep up with Mike on the jungle gym.

But inevitably, the catalog of Tommy's virtues was blotted by overlapping tales of the behavior his father described half jokingly as his "delinquency." Tommy had a girlfriend a couple of houses away, and he totally ignored his parents' insistence that he tell them whenever he planned to visit her. "I have chased him all over the neighborhood," his mother said. He similarly ignored warnings about walking too close to a nearby pond. He left the yard so often that they were wondering whether it would destroy his psyche if they put him on a leash. He got into his father's fishing gear in the garage, which they had thought was well beyond his reach, and ran screaming into the house after hooking himself in the hand. He frequently climbed onto the stove and countertop to get into high cabinets. He had learned to unlock doors. The other day, when his father happened to come by for lunch, Tommy got into the parked car and turned the key to start the engine. "He is one overwhelming, exhausting little boy," his mother concluded.

Good Grief

In line with all of my clients, Tommy's parents had read up on their problem before deciding to seek outside help. One of the books they cited was filled with the kind of short, pithy, often alliterative slogans that one associates with bad advertising. (A prime example is the fiction of the "Terrible Twos.") Under the subject of destructive behavior, for instance, it counseled that when a child does awful things to property or other people, it's time to "get curious, not furious." Try to understand, the book admonished, why the child acts in ways that cause such grief for others. What is he feeling when he steps on the cat's tail? What are the issues behind his clogging the toilet with his brother's teddy bear and then flushing it to overflowing?

This harks back to the story of the psychologist's son, in Chapter 2, who smashed a toy fire truck onto a guest's leg and opened a gash from knee to ankle. The father's concern was all for the child, with none at all for the victim. I told them I thought that this kind of advice was misleading both to the parents, who appeared to be getting the blame, and to the child for whom the parents' response is a reinforcement and an incentive to repeat the destructive behavior.

Several other books dismissed the atrocities as nothing more than a phase. Everybody knows about the Terrible Twos—hardly worth talking about. It's so ephemeral, they tell us, that by the time you finish listing the offenses, your child will have outgrown that brief stage and will be ready to enroll in the Scouts or the Junior Chamber of Commerce. But what do they say to a parent whose child is 3, like Tommy, or 4 or 5, and the punching, breaking, tearing, fire-truck smashing, and other forms of destruction once written off to the Terrible Twos still haven't stopped?

One answer is found in another bestseller that recommends renaming these behaviors, presumably in the hope that they will become more tolerable. In this enlightened newspeak, the Terrible Twos become the Terrific Twos. What is supposed to change, besides the name, is not the behavior, which remains as destructive as ever, but our attitude toward it. It's terrific, the author says, because it's normal. As this philosophy migrates upward on the developmental ladder, we can look forward to a new body of adult laws encouraging, rather than condemning, such natural foibles as Awesome Arson, Marvelous Mayhem, and Happy Homicide.

Collateral Damage Control

I helped Tommy's parents draw up a list of their goals in trying to change the kinds of behavior that were giving them such grief. Their first objective, they quickly agreed, was to keep him safe. Safe from running into the street or too close to the pond, as well as from playing with fishing poles or spraying air freshener into his eyes. They wanted to end the kinds of behavior that were destructive to others, like with the onions, the wall writing, and the liquid soap, and also the teasing and taunting that provoked his anxious parents into pleading with him or chasing him all over the neighborhood. They wanted to be able to go to McDonald's and sit through a whole meal without the fear that when Tommy was ready to leave, he'd start to scream and throw food at the other customers.

Later we made a corollary list of the new things that Tommy would have to learn in order for the parents to achieve those goals. He would have to learn that we don't always get our way and that taking disappointment calmly is an integral part of leading a happy life. The new Tommy would think of other people and their needs. I asked the parents if they considered their son hyperactive. "Well, he can sit down and watch Aladdin movies for three hours," the father said. "The only time he's hyper is when he isn't getting what he wants or when he has to wait for something. His attitude then is, the hell with everyone else—the only one I care about is me." So, we wrote on the second list, "Learn that other people live with him in this world and that he has to respect their needs, feelings, and wishes."

Although Tommy got along pretty well with the neighbors and the other kids in his life, the problem of his destructive behavior wasn't just between him and his parents. I learned that the older brother, Mike, thought everything Tommy did was wonderful and cheered him on. He constantly relived Tommy's past peccadilloes, reminding relatives and friends at every opportunity of such antics as the onions on the rug. "You should have seen Mom," he'd tell his audience. "She was like, 'No, Tommy, no—puhleeeze!'"—and then he would roll on the floor with laughter. "Wow, was that ever cool!" Both sets of grandparents professed a limited degree of sympathy for the fact that this destructive behavior created problems for the parents; they all tried to convince them that it was a phase and they'd be laughing about it in their old age. Sure, little Tommy was "a handful," but it was said more in admiration than with any misgivings or regrets. They encouraged Mike's storytelling and laughed right along with him.

Tommy's mother and father had no trouble understanding that Michael's boosterism and their own parents' amusement made it difficult for their little boy to change, because these other family members were rewarding the precise behaviors we were trying to bring to an end. Tommy's extreme defiance was his way of saying, "I'm a big boy. I won't listen to you. You can't tell me what to do." And the endorsement from his brother and his grandparents told him he was right. So, what the parents needed to do was find other ways of making Tommy feel grown up, not for the destructive behavior, but for behavior that really deserved their approval and support.

I told them about the diary and guided them through what went in it. We agreed they would stop playing the chasing game, which was just as much a reward as his brother's storytelling or the grandparents' laughter. We went through the rules for time-out: to be used only for dangerous or destructive behaviors, only in the home, and with consequences to Michael if he interfered with the punishment.

The behaviors the mother noted in the diary included Tommy's using the toilet properly, saying please and thank you, washing and drying his hands before meals, sharing his toys with friends, and helping pick up

> **B**oth sets of grandparents professed a limited degree of sympathy for the fact that this destructive behavior created problems for the parents; they all tried to convince them that it was a phase and they'd be laughing about it in their old age.

his playroom. In later weeks he wiped up his ice cream after a spill, helped his mother make orange juice, used the toilet before going into the pool, and walked to the car without objection when it was time to go home from a party.

Each time, after a couple of hours, the mother or father would remind him in careful detail what he had done, explain why it was of value, and then share ten or fifteen minutes of special time with him. Tommy was no less creative, no less adorable, no less the apple of his brother's and his grandparents' eyes. What was different was the new reason for everyone's approval: not that little Tommy was an uncontrollable accident that happened with distressing frequency, but instead that he was growing up.

Little Big Man

Tommy's parents came to my office for a total of six visits, between late May and the end of July, eleven years ago. I called today to ask them how they felt about the experience from the perspective of more than a decade. "Telling him he was a big boy was 100 percent the key to changing his behavior," his mother told me. "Until you told us that we had to make him feel grown-up, I hadn't realized how much I had been doing up until then to keep him a baby. He was our last child, and I used to refer to him as 'my little guy.' I stopped doing that eleven years ago. We did what you told us to do right to the letter, and it worked wonderfully. The upheaval and chaos are gone, and we've had a pleasant, positive home ever since. Tom is 14 now, but things aren't better just because he's older. It wasn't a phase he was going through or something he would have outgrown anyway. You helped us to see that he was acting that way because the whole family was making a huge mistake in the way we thought about him and in the way we treated him. He changed because we changed."

23

Defiance/Aggression

Sam is a boy of 4 who puts his hands over his ears and sings a loud song whenever his parents tell him something he doesn't want to hear—which is frequently. Not only does he usually refuse to go to bed on time, nominally at seven, but also he often manages to stretch things out to as late as eleven or even midnight.

Two days before his parents' first visit, however, Sam had gone to bed at six. That's because just before, at the supper table, he had deliberately held a cup of milk in a threatening mode at the end of his outstretched arm, and when his mother saw what he was doing and warned him not to spill it, he promptly turned his hand and splashed the milk all over the kitchen floor. Actually, that wasn't the event that precipitated (appropriate verb) his early retirement. It was what he did next, after his mother had cleaned up the mess, all the while telling him what a problem he had created, and had served him a second cup with a stern warning that if he did it again, she would be very upset.

Now, unless she were clairvoyant, how could she possibly have guessed what would happen? (I make a little joke.)

In the spirit of full disclosure, it should be stipulated—as she did—that there were already numerous other clues pointing to the probability of a second deliberate spill. Sam's mother reported, for example, that if she told him not to touch the cat, he was certain to touch the cat, and he would look at her to make sure she was watching and would smile while he did it. Despite such blatant defiance, he almost always tried to excuse his aggressive behavior with one of three standard rejoinders: it was an accident; his older brother did it; or he was sorry, and he'd never do it again. All were equally false and had the same purpose: to escape consequence. When these responses inevitably failed, his fallback was to place his hands over his ears and sing or yell in order to drown out the words he didn't want to hear.

In addition to this defiance, the mother told me he was often angry when he didn't get his way. He would raise his fist threateningly and call his mother or father "a stupid booby." Occasionally, he would say he was going to chop off their heads. He hit people and threw things, and on his first day of preschool, just two weeks before this visit to my office, he had clamped his hands over his ears and shouted repeatedly at his teacher, "You're not my parents and you can't tell me what to do!"

Open-and-Shut Cases

The books on "problem children" that Sam's parents had read before coming to see me were unanimous in urging them to try to understand their child's feelings rather than focus on his unacceptable actions. Aggressive, defiant behavior offers just one more example of how Freud and post-Freudian psychology have set the world on its head. How does a child learn to act like an adult with that kind of incentive to remain just the way he is? Imagine serial killer Ted Bundy in a court where the judge charges the jury to disregard the evidence of his crimes and try instead to understand what terrible provocation drove this charming, handsome young lawyer to murder all those innocent women.

There is another court story, equally apropos, about a middle-aged man who was arrested for shooting seagulls from a fish pier on Cape Cod. It was a pretty open-and-shut case—dozens of witnesses, a car full of dead birds, and the smoking gun still in the man's hand when the police arrived. The judge said, "I should throw the book at you. The penalty for shooting a gull is $500, which means you owe $20,500." The defendant stood with head bowed but otherwise showed no reaction. Just as he was about to pass sentence, the judge made the same kind of mistake that the advice books make. He asked the man what he possibly could have been thinking at the time of his rampage. Were there some extenuating circumstances, anything that hadn't come out in the hearing, that might warrant a degree of clemency? For the first time, the shooter raised his head and looked the judge straight in the eye.

"Well, your honor," he began, "I am a family man, a trained engineer with two degrees from MIT, and until six months ago I was director of manufacturing for Screwball Industries down in Woods Hole. Last year they

> Imagine serial killer Ted Bundy in a court where the judge charges the jury to disregard the evidence of his crimes and try instead to understand what terrible provocation drove this charming, handsome young lawyer to murder all those innocent women.

went out of business. There's not much else in my line on the Cape, so I've been out of work ever since. I have seven children, ranging from a preschooler to three in college." As the saga continued, the man wove a tale of splendid character, high intentions, incredible bad luck, and desperate need. The dead seagulls, he concluded, were to feed his wife and children, who otherwise would starve.

The judge pulled out a red polka-dot bandana to dab at his eyes and loudly blow his nose, apparently oblivious to the fact that this recitation included no personal responsibility for the wrongdoing at the fish pier. "My heavens, man," he finally interrupted. "Say no more. The fine is waived, and the sentence is suspended. You are free to go."

Like the understanding father of a destructive child, he had managed to look beyond the evidence of the crime to the motives in the defendant's heart. But as the engineer walked out of the courtroom, the judge called after him, "Wait! One last question. I know I'll think about this all night unless I ask you now. What does a seagull taste like?"

The man stopped with his hand on the courtroom door and cocked his head thoughtfully. Clearly he had nothing more to fear from the judge, and he could afford to be gracious, even collegial. "Well, your honor, that depends on what they eat. At first, I shot the gulls down at the town dump, but frankly they tasted a lot like garbage. I analyzed the situation—I'm an engineer, you know—and that's why I wound up at the pier. Those birds follow the commercial fishing boats, and they get nothing but good, fresh seafood."

The judge nodded supportively, but he was obviously waiting for more. He had given up all pretense of neutrality and was now acting as an eager abettor. "Yes, yes," he prodded. "But the gulls from the pier—what do *they* taste like?"

The engineer looked more thoughtful than ever, fixing his gaze at a point high above the judge's head as he searched his mind for the exact words. "Delicate but rich," he pronounced at last. "Subtle, yet with the slightest hint of game. It's a flavor all its own." As the judge continued nodding, the man finally came up with the definitive comparison. "Based on my experience in a wide range of cuisine in the far corners of the world . . . I would place it somewhere between the flavor of an American eagle and a spotted owl."

Common Mistakes All Around

Based on my own experience with a wide range of children from all economic levels, races, and social strata, the reason for defiant, aggressive behavior is almost always nothing more than that the child wants to be treated as a grown-up. Striving to be a big boy is not a diagnosis or a pathology; it's normal, and it's healthy. What was wrong in Sam's case was, first, that he was making a common childhood mistake in how he went about trying to get that result. Worse even was that his parents didn't know how to respond to that behavior without giving Sam the impression that it worked.

They also manufactured a roster of extenuating circumstances in Sam's recent life by which they initially had explained away his transgressions, until the actions became so troublesome that they sought professional help. A year ago the family had moved about a mile to another home within the same city, and the parents assumed the defiance was a result of that relocation. Another was that old standby, that their little boy was experiencing a delayed onset of the Terrible Twos.

The goals I developed with the parents included the following points:

1. Get Sam to bed on time and to sleep.
2. Have him continue in preschool without antagonizing and challenging his teacher.
3. Teach him to listen.

4. No more tantrums.
5. Teach him to express his likes and dislikes without using his fists, threatening his parents, shutting them out with the hands-over-the-ears trick, or using nasty language.

The parents described another side to Sam's character that increased the likelihood that those goals would be achieved. Most of the time—and almost all of the time prior to the past year—he was affectionate, responsive, smart, funny, a quick learner, and a delight to be with. When I explained the diary, the ABCD response, time-outs, and the rest of the program, his mother quickly accepted the logic of the approach, but she said she had a serious misgiving. What if he figured out their motives for giving him this special attention, especially the reinforcements that followed the notation of positive behaviors in the diary?

I told her this was unlikely to happen, and in any event it wouldn't make a bit of difference. The reason positive reinforcement works so well is that children enjoy it. Regardless of how creative Sam may be in figuring out how to get things to go his way, there was little incentive for him to use those skills when things were just right. On the outside chance that he did "see through" to the larger purpose of his parents' new appreciation and attentiveness, I told her there was nothing wrong with admitting the truth. She should tell Sam that she and his father were proud and happy when their son acted so grown-up and that they enjoyed reliving the good moments with him as much as they hoped he did.

Ready, Steady, Go

In the coming weeks, there were many such moments to relive. Sam cleaned his room without being asked; he told his mother he did it so she wouldn't have to. He told his father that he looked at his picture one morning when his father was at work, because he loved him. He helped his older brother look for a lost piggy bank, unprompted. He said he

> The reason positive reinforcement works so well is that children enjoy it.

had stayed in bed four nights in a row because he knew it made his mother happy when he was a "big boy." He made his grandmother a card after she had surgery, "so she will feel better." He helped a little girl at school rebuild a block tower that another student had accidentally knocked over. When the family traveled to a local farm and then had to turn back because it was too busy, he took the disappointment calmly.

Over the following weeks, his behavior showed a steady turn for the better. With his aggression and defiance no longer being rewarded, they came to an end. Sam was as glad as anyone for the change. And as I predicted, he never bothered to wonder why.

24

ANGER

ARTHUR IS A BOY of 21 months whose mother told me he had a "bad temper." She said he banged his head—on the tray of his high chair, on the floor, on the footboard of his bed—three or four times a week. The most common reason for the behavior, she thought, was that things weren't going his way, but sometimes it also might be that Arthur couldn't figure out what he wanted. He was just learning to put sentences together, and as with any child—as well as more than a few adults—the words that came out often expressed something different from his intentions.

She offered an illustration from just two hours earlier, when she had been preparing Arthur's breakfast. He asked for a muffin, and then he said to his mother, "Cut." Although she dutifully cut off a sliver of muffin and offered to place it in his mouth, he pushed her away angrily and banged his head on the breakfast table. She deduced from this that he had actually meant to stop her from cutting. He was either frustrated at not having the language skills to communicate what he wanted or angry at her for ignoring his wishes. "Arthur likes big things," she explained. "He likes a whole muffin or a whole bagel, and I should have known." She added that when she picked him up and told him he could have the whole muffin, the rage ceased, and he was fine.

The head banging had been going on since Arthur's first birthday. Because of food allergies, he was seriously underweight and also was well below the average height for a child his age. He had difficulty dressing and undressing and was unusually shy. She said he took a half hour to "warm up" before he started to have a normal interaction with other children, even those he had met before. He pretty much set his own hours for going to bed and getting up, and he frequently woke his parents by wandering into their bedroom in the middle of the night.

Arthur's other big offensive weapon was food throwing. He didn't generally react negatively when food was taken away from him, but when something he disliked was placed in front of him, he would often pick it up and fling it against the wall or onto the floor. His mother supposed that this angry reaction owed to his food allergies, but even so, she hoped he would learn a better way to express his preferences than flying into an automatic, self-destructive rage.

Multiple Choices

In an attempt to get to the bottom of the problem on her own, the mother said she had bought a book of baby faces showing different moods and expressions: happiness, anger, hurt, curiosity, and so on, which had been designed by a psychologist to help parents communicate with children who had not yet mastered language. She sat down with Arthur and asked him to identify the face that best reflected what he was feeling when he banged his head or threw food. She explained to him that this was very bad behavior and that the next time he felt like head banging, he should stomp instead. I suppose this strategy was an attempt to limit the risk of brain damage, but I explained to her why it was a mistake. First, she was telling Arthur that unacceptable behavior was OK after all, just as long as he didn't hurt himself. Second, she was rewarding the head banging with attention and inappropriate permission, guaranteed to produce repeat performances—perhaps with an added dance act to make things more interesting. And third, her response to Arthur's rage was to take on the role of therapist, when what he needed was not an analyst, not an enabler, not an approver, but a parent.

Following the pattern of most parents with a difficult child, Arthur's mother told me that she and her husband had read everything they could find on the subject. They had even gone a step further, attending two ninety-minute programs, in company with twenty people like themselves, on the subject of the angry child. Applying what they learned, they had whittled down the problem behavior to five or six probable causes. The most likely one was that little Arthur was going through a difficult phase. They heard that all children regress just before they make the next development step—and that given the ferocity of Arthur's rages, they could expect great things from the boy. Another response was that Arthur's anger was the symptom (there's that medical model again) of an emotional problem, and it would either go away or get a whole lot worse—a fairly risk-free prognosis for the therapist. They were told that angry children can't help their behavior, that it's a natural, inevitable part of childhood, so it's up to the parents to get over their confused and impatient reaction. I've heard that malarkey so often that I refer to it as "grin-and-bear-it parenting." The best catchphrase of all was that old standby of blaming the behavior on the Terrible Twos. By that explanation, Arthur's behavior wasn't a problem after all; he was just precocious.

How is it, do you suppose, I asked Arthur's parents, that most children on Hopi Indian reservations in the Southwest go through the twos without ever exhibiting any of the so-called symptoms of this "normal, inevitable" stage of developmental blowout? We also see children from many other diverse and widely separated parts of the globe—Asia and France, for example—who equally tend to be happy, well adjusted, and extremely well behaved at those same ages.

One of the more disturbing things Arthur's parents had been told during the two ninety-minute programs was that their little boy might have a temperament problem. Our temperament is presumed to be something each of us is born with, so the assumption in such judgments is that there is nothing one can do to make it better. Be more sensitive, they were advised, more sympathetic. Poor little Arthur was born that way. I have actually heard parents say to a difficult, angry child, "I know you can't help it, sweetheart, but . . . ." And when parents complain to psychologists that they have tried everything they were told to do, but nothing has improved, the stock reply is, "You just have to live through it. Sometimes you won't know whether you've done the right thing until years later." The consumer gets a better warranty than that on a used car.

Hanging Out Is Out

At the most fundamental level, there is only one universal reason for the Terrible Twos, and that is that parents have accepted as a given in life that they must act as therapists to their children. Discipline is important, they are told, but first and foremost the parent must acknowledge the child's feelings. The problem with this advice is that when the subject is unbridled rage, acknowledging those kinds of feelings is an open invitation to more of the same. We've all heard that touchy-feely advice of the 1960s when adults were

At the most fundamental level, there is only one universal reason for the Terrible Twos, and that is that parents have accepted as a given in life that they must act as therapists to their children.

encouraged in their anger to "just let it all hang out." Giving permission to continue in outrageously unacceptable behavior, which was a mantra of Freudian psychology back in that era, was so patently absurd that it quickly became a joke. Today, suggesting to someone who is in a rage to "let it all hang out" is a gentle if ironic way of saying the person is acting foolishly.

I explained to Arthur's mother that the first responsibility of a parent is to teach, and then I made a list with her, headed "What Does Arthur Need to Learn?":

1. To use words
2. To be in charge of his life, to start feeling independent
3. That we live in a world in which we can't always have our way
4. To get on a reasonable schedule of sleeping, waking, dressing, and eating

Everything the mother had told me indicated that her son wanted to be in control, to have a proper sense of autonomy as a reward for growing up. The challenge would be to teach him how to earn that control without rage, without head banging, and without throwing food.

We went over the diary and the ABCD response. Because of his history of eating problems, I warned her against coaxing him to take food, as this only rewarded his refusal-to-eat behaviors. I also told her to stop discussing his feelings when he was angry and to stop using the face book. When anger is followed by a lesson, that lesson will only be perceived as a reward for the anger.

We then made a list of goals:

1. No head banging
2. Eating more and better
3. Bedtime without problems
4. Dressing and undressing without problems

"Why, I Oughtta . . . "

Over the following weeks, Arthur's mother dealt with the head banging and food throwing with time-outs, as she systematically nurtured the kinds of behavior with which we wanted to see them replaced. It is always a mistake to dismiss this kind of rage behavior as a phase. Exhibit A is the Three Stooges, but we all know other, real-life adults who have only slightly less difficulty than infants in controlling their anger. However, it was obvious at

When anger is followed by a lesson, that lesson will only be perceived as a reward for the anger.

the outset that a principal source of the frustration that fed little Arthur's anger was his difficulty expressing himself in words. The inability to speak is a problem that always diminishes with experience and with passing time, and in that regard Arthur was no different from almost everybody else.

The reason he got over the head banging, which reduced in frequency within the first couple of weeks and eventually stopped entirely, along with the food throwing, was not that he had simply grown older or that he continued learning how to speak. It wasn't that his mother finally found a happy face in the book with which he could identify, or that his parents decided to sit back and ride out the storm. He got over it because his parents stopped treating him as therapists and began to relate to him in the way nature intended, as his teachers.

25

THE FRIENDLESS CHILD

❊⸺❊

KAREN, WHO JUST TURNED 6, was about to enter first grade at the end of the summer. On a family trip to a theme park in Pennsylvania, her older sister asked her if she was getting excited about finally going to "real school." Karen's answer shocked the sister. "No. I want to go back to kindergarten instead."

The older sister said she couldn't believe it. "But, *everyone* wants to grow up! What about your friends? They're all going on to the first grade. Nobody else is repeating. Why do you want to stay a baby?"

"Why not?" Karen answered. She added as an afterthought, "Besides, I don't have any friends." Their mother was listening from the front seat, and she was less surprised than the older sister by Karen's attitude.

Breaking the Charm

Unlike with the other children in the family, Karen's primary response to almost everything was to complain. A year before, when she had gone off to kindergarten, her parents had expected that the negative behavior, the whining and faultfinding, would be "socialized out of her" (her mother's phrase, borrowed from a popular book on child psychology). They hoped that after five years as the youngest member of the family, Karen would learn to make and keep friends, but they were disappointed. Although she showed a ready faculty for making friends quickly, she demonstrated a nearly total lack of ability to keep them.

The situation reminded her father of the movie *The Barefoot Contessa*. Humphrey Bogart is told that one of the other characters "could charm the birds right out of the trees." A short time later, following an outrageous offense, Bogart says, "Well, it looks like he's just charmed them right back into the trees."

Despite the parents' hopes, it turned out that Karen acted in first grade pretty much the same way she acted at home, where the negative behaviors were tolerated because of her status as the baby in the house. In school, however, she ran into a far different reception from her new peers. She met several children she liked, and they liked her, but in every case, after a very short time, whenever she invited one or more of them to her house, they began to find excuses not to come. What it came down to was they didn't like to be bossed around, and when things didn't go exactly Karen's way, she would burst into tears and run up to her bedroom, leaving them to fend for themselves or, worse, feeling they had to explain themselves to Karen's mother.

That summer, when the family joined up with cousins at the theme park, Karen began relating to them much the same way as she had with the kids in kindergarten. In order to avoid favoring one child over another or leaving anybody out, it was agreed the kids would be assigned partners on a rotating basis for each of the rides and attractions. Karen, though, had already decided which of the children she was interested in being with, and she noisily refused to alternate. When the older members of the family enforced the rules, Karen found herself paired with the cousins or siblings she had noisily rejected a few minutes earlier, and she started to cry and complain so loudly that her mother pulled her out of the group. "Why do you behave this way?" she demanded, more in frustration than in anger.

She answered, "Because I don't want to sit with them."

Karen was dealing with the prospect of first grade with a similar kind of circular logic. She didn't want to go because she didn't want to go. "I want to be in kindergarten again."

> **M**ost of the current bestsellers on parenting get it right when they tell us that the friendless child is the product of defective behavior patterns that have been allowed to expand beyond the family.

The Parents' Merry-Go-Round

Before coming to see me, the mother had spoken with Karen's first-grade teacher in the hope of getting some insights or advice on how to deal with the problem. The teacher wasn't much more help than Karen. "It looks as if she doesn't want to grow up. Some kids take longer than others. I'm sure she'll get over it as soon as she's in the new school. But I guess she still wants to play."

After that, the mother headed for the local Barnes & Noble. Two weeks later, with school just days away, she decided to make the telephone call that brought her to my office.

As is typical, after describing her daughter's problem in the first few minutes of that initial meeting, she told me about some of the books she had found that touch on friendless children. Most of the current bestsellers on parenting get it right when they tell us that the friendless child is the product of defective behavior patterns that have been allowed to expand beyond the family. Too bad they come up so short on the advice they offer for how to cope with it. One book says that friendship problems are the natural curse of the middle child and that it's the job of the parents to compensate by lavishing middle children with extra attention and love. Well, Karen was not a middle child, and having friendship problems is in no way connected to birth order. In fact, in my experience, very little in childhood is reliably explained on the basis of birth order.

Another book Karen's parents had toted home advised them how to tutor kids in the neighborhood on ways in which they could help compensate for their child's deficit. It is expecting far too much of a child's peers to respond to rude behaviors and slights, as that particular book suggests, by smiling sweetly and saying, "It's all right. I understand." Children are no more likely to do that than to say, "Let's talk about why it hurts," or, "How about if I rub your eyebrows?" As if it weren't enough to urge the parents to be therapists, this expert wants to recruit the entire neighborhood to that same lofty calling. Not only is this advice absurdly unworkable, but also I can't imagine a quicker way to brand a child who has friendship problems as a loser.

The Real World

I told Karen's mother that her child's peers couldn't be expected to practice psychiatry and didn't function in the dream world of unprovable, unworkable theory. Rather, they were concerned entirely with reality-based consequences. Therefore, if Karen wanted to hold on to the friendship of her peers beyond the first few interactions with them, she would have to change the way she treated them. If she didn't and instead continued failing to measure up to their expectations, the consequence would not be endless patience, false assurances that all is well, encouragement in her repeated failures, eyebrow rubs, or years of therapy. The consequence, fast and perhaps final, would be more rejection.

The goals we set for Karen were as follows:

1. Be happier, not only with her life and her friends but also with herself.
2. Stop the crying and whining.
3. Learn to be a friend.
4. Learn how to maintain friendships.

I told her that Karen's comment about wanting to not grow up indicated that she felt it paid off to be a baby. Babies get attention, people see to their needs, they often get their way, and they get more love than big girls. Those are the things Karen wants.

So, how do the parents of a child like Karen go about changing her mind-set? We talked about the diary, recording specific examples of friendship behavior (taking turns in a game, saying good-bye when leaving, sharing, helping, praising other children), thinking-of-others behavior, taking disappointment calmly, the opposite of the self-centeredness that was causing her problems. When the mother returned a week later, she had recorded several such instances. Karen took turns in a game. She shared her doll with Melissa. She allowed Fran to play the games she wanted to play. She thoughtfully moved over in the bed to make space for a sister who was sharing her room for the night. The mother summarized, "We actually had a pretty good week."

> When parents start consciously looking for friend behaviors, they are going to notice more of them.

I told her that wasn't unusual. When parents start consciously looking for friend behaviors, they are going to notice more of them. And when they reinforce those behaviors with praise and special time with their child, they will happen with increasing frequency. Moreover, using the ABCD method four to eight times weekly builds self-esteem, making Karen proud of herself for the behaviors that have won her the praise and the attention that she had previously attained only by being childish.

Friends Indeed

As of this writing, which is only a year later, Karen has returned to school, this time in second grade. Many of the same children who shied away from her in first grade have renewed their initial friendship, and she has made new friends as well.

This time, she greeted the new school year with the excitement and enthusiasm her older sister had been hoping for.

26

HITTING, BITING, THROWING

❦⸺⸻❦

BURT IS A 2½-year-old boy whose mother describes him as "angry, defiant, and uncooperative." The three principal reasons for this assessment were that he had hit her on several occasions with his fists, had bitten an older sister and the family dog numerous times, and at one time or another had thrown just about everything in the house that he was strong enough to lift. His father said he is looking forward to seeing his son play in the World Series or take up a career in prizefighting; at the very least, he would make an extremely successful bill collector.

What, I asked, were the most common occasions for these behaviors? As it happened, on the morning his parents first came to see me, he had raised his fist to his mother just because she asked him to put on his shorts. He didn't actually hit her—in fact, he threatened violence far more often than he actually followed up—but he had punched her enough times previously that the mother said she was frightened every time he made a fist. She also told me he screamed and told her to go away when she asked him to do things. The objects he threatened to throw—or actually did throw—included crayons, a dump truck, the engine of a toy train, books, blocks, story cards, and plastic cups. He hit his maternal grandmother several times, once so hard that it raised a lump on her forehead. She lives in the same town and visited regularly, but after that one she stayed away for a whole week. Most of the time, the specific provocations were requests by the parents or grandmother that he pick up after himself or do some other small thing that he decided he didn't want to do.

Laugh till It Hurts

The parenting books that Burt's mother and father had read enjoined them to talk with their child, to hug and support him after such behavior, to use logic and reason, and to appeal to his empathy. I always have to stop myself from laughing when I hear that word in the context of this type of behavior. What empathy are they talking about? The parents didn't bring along any examples of suggested dialogue, so I'll use a little invention to get the point across:

"There, there, sweetheart, you must be very upset to have thrown that creamed spinach all over the kitchen wall. Give Mommy a kiss."

"You'll become very unpopular if you continue to bite everyone the way you do. How about showing a little restraint?"

"Now, I want you to stop hitting your grammie for a moment and consider how it would feel to have someone do that to you."

The flaw with the first response, of course, is that sympathy instead of discipline, and hugs instead of punishment, are rewards; they only reinforce the objectionable behavior and virtually guarantee that it will be repeated. What's wrong with the second answer is that popularity is not a top priority for children who bite people, and neither is restraint—plus, if they were all that logical, they wouldn't be doing it in the first place. Ditto for the third reply: hitting isn't about empathy; it's about hurting people.

When a parent reads that kind of advice for dealing with violent behavior, a good test is whether it would work with Hannibal Lecter, the murderous psychiatrist in *The Silence of the Lambs*, whose childhood taste for biting developed into a serious, life-long, bad habit. This isn't to suggest that children who bite, throw things, or hit people are vicious sociopaths or that they're mentally ill, because almost certainly they are neither. What they do have in common with Dr. Lecter is a learned pattern of behavior in which logic, reason, and empathy are clearly absent and for which displays of affection and acceptance are absolutely the wrong response.

> There's no reason for a mother—or a grandmother—to take a punch in the face with a smile, or for an older sister or even a dog to accept being bitten as just normal, boys-will-be-boys behavior.

A Different View

The first thing I tell parents of kids like Burt is why their children sometimes hit, bite, and throw. They're trying to act bigger than they really are. Their behavior reflects their frustration at being little and powerless and is an attempt to beat the clock in the race to grow up. We then set up some specific goals for how we would like to see that behavior improve by giving the child better ways of being truly grown-up. In Burt's case, those goals were the following:

1. Less defiance
2. More cooperation
3. No hitting, no biting, and no throwing things

Burt's mother told me that she felt guilty that her child's behavior made her so angry. I told her that feeling angry was perfectly normal—it would make anyone angry. There's no reason for a mother—or a grandmother—to take a punch in the face with a smile, or for an older sister or even a dog to accept being bitten as just normal, boys-will-be-boys behavior. She also said she was worried that because they hadn't figured out how to successfully cope with the situation, it was only getting worse.

We discussed the role of parent as teacher and then made up a list of the things Burt had to learn in order for his behavior to change for the better:

1. Be thoughtful of other people's feelings, needs, and wishes.
2. Handle disappointment calmly.
3. Develop self-control.

When the mother returned the following week with the pages of her diary, they included an incident in which she'd praised Burt for breaking off a piece of his raisin cookie and sharing it with his father. So far, so good. But then she'd undone the praise by asking why he didn't show the same generosity to his grammie, who was now back in the picture, and to herself. "How do you think it makes Grammie feel when you don't show her the same generosity you showed your father? I'm pleased you shared, but I'm disappointed you didn't think of us as well." Instead of looking proud of the praise, he acted disappointed and confused by the criticism. Once again, I explained the need for absolute, undiluted praise and emphasized that mixing it with criticisms did more harm than good.

Another problem with the way that the parents had previously responded to Burt's transgressions was in what they regarded as a time-out. Whenever he threw a tantrum, which was approximately every two hours, they would send him to his room and close the door. Burt was so used to this response that he seldom objected; in fact, he usually reacted as though he was pleased with the change of scene. Not only did this "punishment" get him out of whatever it was that caused the blowup, but also his bedroom had a television, a chest full of toys and games, a radio, and a second-floor view of the Boston skyline that included the traffic into and out of Logan Airport. The time-out was equivalent to a stay in a well-appointed resort.

> Every time children hear about what will happen next time or are asked to think about anything, they know they're off the hook for whatever just happened.

In place of sending him on that kind of vacation four or five times a day, they would have to institute an effective practice. I explained the procedure with the chair and the neutral environment, which meant no toys or games, no TV or radio, no view of the outside world, and *no conversation*. The new time-out was to be used only for serious misbehaviors: tantrums, hitting, throwing anything in anger, biting, destructive behavior such as knocking objects off of tables, or major defiance.

There would be no more warnings or second chances. As soon as he committed an infraction, he was immediately placed in the time-out chair, with only one sentence of communication from the parent: "We do not bite." Or "We do not throw things." There was nothing about "If you do that one more time . . . " or "Now, Burt, I want you to think about what you just did." Every time children hear about what will happen next time or are asked to think about anything, they know they're off the hook for whatever just happened. *No explanation* beyond the one-line admonition—*"We do not . . . "*—that names the offense. *No sympathy. No apologies*—"Gee, Burt, this hurts me more than it hurts you"—and *no back talk.*

For more particulars on time-outs, diaries, and the ABCD method of positive reinforcement, see Chapters 14, 15, 16, and 17.

Seeing Is Believing

Burt is now 9. When I called his mother recently for an update, she told me the results had been nearly immediate. Within a month, Burt had gone from five tantrums a day to nearly none. The time-outs diminished accordingly, and the occasions for the ABCDs became more numerous and rewarding to them both. She gave up the diary after a few months, but they still used the reinforcement technique of reconstructing the positive behavior and telling him why it is valued, followed by special time together. They don't do it because they have to. They do it because they love it. Burt is now cooperative and free of anger, has good manners, refers to himself as his mother's "helper guy" and is the apple of his grandmother's eye.

His mother recalled that in the next several months after her final visit seven years ago, instead of her having to tell Burt which behaviors were unacceptable, she frequently heard him say same the same words to himself—"We do not . . . ." And then, whatever it was, he didn't. "We could actually see him changing before our eyes," she said. "It has been a blessing for us all."

27

SCREAMING

THE FIRST TIME WE MET, Warren's mother told me she'd had a dream. It was like a film, set in an old-time Hollywood casting office. There is a timid knock at the door, and after a moment her 4-year-old son enters the room, nervously crosses the plush carpet, and pushes a résumé across the top of a great mahogany desk. A classic, cigar-chomping movie mogul complete with pith helmet, hunting jacket, megaphone, and a riding crop picks the résumé up, glances briefly at the single page (obviously, it's short), shifts the stogie from one side of his mouth to the other, and says, "Warren? *Warren?* Well, never mind, kid; we can change that. So, whaddya do?"

Warren is so short that he can barely see the speaker. He stands on tiptoe for a better view, smiles shyly, takes a breath so long and deep that his face turns purple and veins pop out on his forehead, and answers: "I SCREAM! I'M A SCREAMER! I SCREAM IN RESTAU-RANTS, IN SUPERMARKETS, ON THE BUS, IN THE ELEVA-

TOR, EVEN IN CHURCHES! I DRIVE PEOPLE CRAZY WITH MY SCREAMING!"

The movie mogul is driven back into his chair. "Wow!" he says, adjusting his cracked eyeglasses and smoothing his ascot. "I'm impressed. I mean, I am *really* impressed."

"I can do it again," Warren offers.

"No, no, no, no, no."

Once More with Feeling

No question, Warren has a big talent. He started screaming before he turned 2, and after the first few performances, his mother took him to a pediatrician. The doctor weighed him, measured him, and looked into his ears, up his nose, and down his throat. "He's fine. Nothing the matter that shows."

"But the screaming—" his anxious mother said. "He's out of control!"

The doctor responded with a "there, there" pat on the shoulder that prodded her toward the reception room and out the front door. "Perfectly normal for his age. He's just not ready to be *in* control. After all, he's not even 2."

She took him back a year later, and the doctor repeated the same assurances almost word for word. "After all, he's only 2." By then she'd had the dream, and it occurred to her that the doctor looked an awful lot like the moviemaker. Less than a month later, Warren turned 3. A year after that, he was 4. There were several more visits to the doctor in the interim, but by then his mother knew better than to bring up the subject of his behavior. The only thing that changed about the screaming was that it got louder. Muscles grow with exercise, and for those two years Warren's vocal cords had been pumping serious iron.

The advice about screaming that the parents had read before calling me was more of the same type of pap they had heard from the pediatrician. One variation was that the screaming child of 3 or more is telling the world that he or she is "stuck" at a level of development, so instead of getting annoyed, parents should respond to the behavior as a cry for help. Another book said it's a temperamental problem and they would have to get used to it: along with the blue eyes and curly hair, it's a feature of the kind of child you've got. A third said screaming is acceptable because it simply signifies that the child has not yet learned to put his needs and feelings into words. Parents are told that they need to help such children learn to express themselves in a more acceptable way and that they do this through logical discussion and gentle persuasion.

The fallacy in all of this, as usual, is that it invents a rational cause for behavior that is absolutely not rational. The reason Warren screamed was that he wanted something. Plenty of adults also raise their voices when they want something, and Warren just took it a few decibels further. "GARY WON'T GIVE ME BACK MY BULLDOZER!" "I DON'T WANT TO PLAY TAG! I WANT TO PLAY HIDE-AND-SEEK!"

Expanding the Repertoire

In addition to the named object or activity, Warren wanted more attention than he figured he was likely to get if he asked at a lower pitch. When his mother was on the telephone, for example, he would tug at the hem of her dress or crawl up onto the hallway table to kiss her and then try hanging from her free arm like a baby chimp. When she was talking with the plumber about a leak under the sink, that was the time he chose to go out to the car and start clicking the garage door up and down until she was forced to run out into the driveway and take away the opener. When his sister Anna was trying to whisper a secret to their mother, he drowned her out by flipping on the disposal. He wanted 100 percent attention, and when he got it, he was fine.

When he didn't, or when something went the wrong way, screaming was not the only weapon in his arsenal. He frequently hit other children, particularly Anna, who was a year older, and sometimes his mother. He liked to roughhouse, and that, too, often quickly escalated to a level beyond the tolerance of his playmates. He pushed other kids to the ground, girls as well as boys, and then he'd drop onto them, screaming "Chunga! Chunga!" like a sumo wrestler. He spent a whole afternoon with his best friend, Webster, fighting, screaming, and throwing balls at him because "WEB ISN'T PLAYING WHAT I WANT TO PLAY!" On other occasions, he had threatened to break something belonging to his mother if she didn't let him have his way. He had also told both his mother and grandmother, "I HATE YOU! I HOPE YOU DIE!"

> **B**eing a big boy means learning how to relate to others, to be more caring, and to take disappointment calmly.

He has a hard time making friends," his mother said. "Kids don't want to play with him because they're afraid of getting hurt. And he doesn't play at all well by himself; he needs somebody all the time."

A New Method of Acting

We made up a list of what Warren had yet to learn: recognizing and honoring the feelings, needs, and wishes of others; that none of us can always have his or her own way; and how to develop self-control. Then

I took his mother through the steps in creating and using the diary, along with the ABCD procedures. All children want attention, I told her, so what we have to do is find ways of giving him attention for the kinds of behavior that build his self-esteem. "We have to give him a new way of thinking of himself as more grown-up. Being a big boy means learning how to relate to others, to be more caring, and to take disappointment calmly. And it means not shouting to get his way or screaming when he doesn't."

The following week she brought in a list of his remarkable accomplishments in just the first seven days. He had let Anna have the only ice cream bar. He surrendered his seat at the computer without complaining when his time was up. He tried dressing all by himself on a couple of mornings, "to help Mom." On an evening when his grandfather, who had a hard time climbing stairs, was babysitting, Warren went up to bed on his own with no hesitation or back talk, after kissing Grandpa good night and saying that he loved him.

There were negative behaviors as well, and the mother relayed that Warren had been given three time-outs. All of them were for screaming. In the past, when Warren had needed discipline, his mother had used an entirely different approach. Several weeks earlier, for example, he had started choking a friend in a game of make-believe that got out of hand. She had physically separated the two boys, forcefully admonished Warren in front of his friend and told him why what he did was wrong and dangerous, and then insisted that he apologize. In the three most recent offenses, however, she made sure there was no one else present but the family, and the only thing she told Warren before sitting him down in the chair was, "We do not scream."

The Reviews Are In

It has been three years since I consulted with Warren's parents, but his mother told me the other day that they have continued the positive reinforcements right up to the present. "The biggest change was in just the first few weeks," she said, "partly because the contrast with his earlier behavior was so noticeable. But the improvement has continued steadily ever since."

I reminded her of the dream in which Warren was auditioning in the casting office, and she laughed. "To tell the truth," she confided, "that dream really scared me, even though I joked about it at the time. I guess the good news/bad news is that Warren's career as a screamer in the movies is never going to happen. Thank God, those days are gone forever."

28

JEALOUSY

◄◦———◦►

WE ALL KNOW STORIES of jealousy. The Bible tells us it was why Cain murdered his brother Abel, and Joseph's brothers were so envious of his coat of many colors that they sold him into slavery. In modern times, a Texas mom contracted for the murder of the mother of her daughter's rival in cheerleading. Even more recent is the "classic" case of little Jenny Hogan.

Jenny's story never made the papers, no songs were written about it, and it lacks the great climactic act—murder, betrayal, conspiracy—that raises the more dramatic tales into the realm of folklore. Besides, at the time I met her parents, she was only 4, and kids that age are not quite yet the stuff of legend. Even so, her particular saga had its moments.

Classicism

I describe Jenny's case as classic, not only because that's the word her parents used at that first visit, but also because they in turn had based that assessment on the highest possible authority, the family doctor. Jenny had been defiant and resistant to discipline from before the time she could talk, with frequent tantrums when things didn't go her way. She stomped, refused to go to bed on time, and angrily threw down toys that she either tired of or couldn't figure out how to use. Before coming to me, the parents had discussed this behavior with their pediatrician, noting that it had worsened somewhat about a year ago, around the time of the birth of her brother, Harry. The learned doctor had smiled knowingly and delivered that one-word critique: "Classic." The classic to which he was referring, of course, was sibling rivalry.

I asked the parents if that was the principal reason why they were in my office. They exchanged looks of mutual uncertainty. "We're not really sure that's the whole problem," the mother said. "Jenny was a handful before her brother came along, and if she got worse afterward, that doesn't necessarily change the basic reasons why she acts that way."

Defining a class of behavior by something that happened after it started is backward logic.

She then told me of a subsequent change in the family that had seemingly influenced their daughter's behavior even more than the birth of the brother. The mother's sister was going through a crisis in her marriage, and they had taken in her 16-month-old son for a few weeks or months, in order to help her out. Jenny's reaction to the arrival of the little cousin was far more obvious jealousy than she had been showing toward baby Harry. In fact, since this outsider had taken up temporary residence in the home, there were some small signs that she may be revising her view of her infant sibling from rival to a fellow traveler and perhaps even an ally.

Backward Logic

I've had a number of parents tell me that a certain class of behavior had become worse since the birth of a younger child, so the old behavior now had a new name: sibling rivalry. The trouble is, it doesn't make sense to attribute Jenny's negative behavior to sibling rivalry just because it increased around the time of her brother's birth; defining a class of behavior by something that happened after it started is backward logic. If little Jenny was doing more screaming, stomping, defying her parents, throwing toys, or whatever since the birth of her brother, it's simply because there was more opportunity and, with the parents' attention now divided by the new child, more incentive.

The cousin could be seen as a kind of substitute sibling as well, I suppose, but it's much more realistic to see him as the parents did, as just one more such incentive for Jenny to interfere with the family's daily life by demanding more and more of their attention.

Jenny's needy nature showed itself in lots of other ways than problems with her brother and cousin. If she hurt herself while playing down the street with neighborhood children, she would come all the way home, waiting until she was within earshot of the house before starting to cry, and then ask her mother to kiss the bump or scratch. She fell frequently and cried so often that her mother called her the Drama Queen. They lived in a part of town not serviced by a school bus, and when her mother drove her to school, Jenny frequently clung to her and whined during the trip in fearful anticipation of the day ahead, and especially of their parting. The whining wasn't restricted to her anxieties, either. If she wanted a glass of chocolate milk, say, instead of making her desire known in a normal voice, she used a plaintive and impatient tone, as though already offended by the lack of instant gratification.

One of the best-known pieces of bad advice on child raising, which is often quoted when an older sibling attacks or slights a younger one,

One of the best-known pieces of bad advice on child raising, which is often quoted when an older sibling attacks or slights a younger one, is the platitude "A child is most in need of love when the child least deserves it." is the platitude "A child is most in need of love when the child least deserves it." That may be a high ideal in some religions, but in terms of how it is most often interpreted in parenting, it's nothing but a huge mistake. The author of that bromide suggests that positive attention and love always mean the same thing, and he calls on parents to reward bad behavior such as jealousy and spite with understanding, hugs, solicitous tsk-tsks, and other forms of inappropriate reinforcement. In cases in which the butt of the bad behavior is a sibling, that kind of parental response is potentially devastating. Not only does it comfort the perpetrator, but it also betrays the victim. Moreover, it sets a model for future behavior that *both* children will most likely find irresistible.

Time Will Tell

The goals we wrote down for Jenny at my first session with her parents were to eliminate the hitting, tantrums, stomping, and defiance and to help her find her way to becoming a happier girl. In order for this to happen, she had to learn self-control; respect for the needs, feelings, and wishes of others (obviously including her little brother, although he was not named); and that we can't always get what we want. I explained how the diary worked and how to reinforce sibling caring, Mother Teresa behaviors, and taking disappointment calmly. As for the jealousy, there was no way for that to coexist with sibling caring, and I told the parents it would be one of the earliest of Jenny's problems to disappear.

When the mother returned the following week, the first behavior she mentioned was the jealousy, which had all but vanished. The number one item she'd entered in her diary was under the heading of sibling caring; Jenny had shared her spaghetti dinner with her little brother and had taught Harry how to roll the noodles onto the fork. The following day, she'd started playing with one of her brother's toys, and when he asked for it, she gave it to him and got another toy for herself. The mother also said the incidences of stomping had dropped from ten times a week to three or four, she cleaned her room when asked, she put her dirty dishes in the sink, and she was calm when it was time for her to leave after playing at a friend's house.

When I asked the mother why these improvements had taken place, she surprised me by answering that it was probably because her sister's son had gone back home to his mother, and as a result, she had been able to spend a lot more one-on-one time with Jenny. I flashed back to several decades earlier, when the psychiatric patient cited in Chapter 16 told the review board that the reason he was up for release after years of confinement was that God had cured him. Maybe God had something to do with it, but the immediate reason he was better was the medicine he had been given, and without it he'd spend the rest of his life under lock and key.

I reminded the mother that she had been keeping a diary of Jenny's positive behaviors, and I asked if she was reinforcing them in the ways I had described. She said that she had been and that every minute of the extra time she had been able to give her daughter in the prior week was the special time prescribed in the program. "Then, it isn't God, after all," I thought to myself. "It's the Thorazine!"

But of course, those were not the words I said aloud. Instead, I told her that if reinforcing the diary behaviors such as being nice to her brother was the reason for the extra time, and the extra time was the reason for the improvements, then whether the nephew stayed or went was beside the point.

29

OUT-OF-CONTROL
BEHAVIOR

◈◦———◦◈

JAYNE'S MOTHER DESCRIBED the problem succinctly just one minute into her first visit. "She's hyper, totally out of control. We can't contain her." Her frustration evoked the cartoon of the harried father clutching a screaming infant and holding up a piece of paper at the admissions desk of a maternity hospital. The receptionist is saying to him, "No, sir, we do not accept returns or exchanges, and besides, that's not a receipt; it's a birth certificate."

The mother told me Jayne seldom listened when asked to do things, often acting as though the parent making the request wasn't even in the room. (Yes, they did test her hearing, and she could hear a pin drop at 100 yards.) She hurts her sister with prodding, poking, pinching, squeezing, and once by biting her—anything to make her cry. She poked a finger in her sister's eye. She frequently yelled at her just to watch her jump, which Jayne considered to be hilarious. When the parents disciplined her for this type of behavior, she sometimes retaliated on the sister with further aggression.

She would throw things, scream at the top of her voice, cry, and tell her parents she hated them. At times she would rather wet her pants than use the bathroom if it meant interrupting a good time.

They said she was particularly hyper at bedtime. (This was the second time they used the word *hyper*, and I asked if they had been to someone who had given their daughter a diagnosis of ADHD. No, it was just that they knew there was a lot of it around, and it certainly described the way she acted.) She would lead them on a chase all around the bedroom, and it was all they could do to get

When it comes to listening to advice, using the toilet, brushing their teeth, or going to bed, a child's logic is that these are the very things that most often get in the way of what life is really about, which is having fun.

her into the bathroom to brush her teeth. One of her favorite delaying tactics was to lie on the floor and go limp. "It isn't a tantrum exactly," her mother said, "because she's laughing. She thinks it's a riot."

I told her that was because it was a game, all the better because she was playing it at her parents' expense.

Outside the home, the contrast in Jayne's behavior was so remarkable that their friends and neighbors would often respond to the parents' stories in stunned disbelief. "They tell us they don't know what we're talking about," the father confirmed. "She plays well with other kids, she's polite and thoughtful—and she's so popular with the adults, there's no way the angelic little girl who visits their house could possibly be such a devil anywhere else."

Seeking Asylum

"The problem may be related to a milk allergy . . . " the mother started to say, but I shook my head.

"Allergies don't turn on and off depending on the people you're with," I pointed out. "This isn't about allergies; it's about learning."

The father said he agreed. He had repeatedly told their daughter that she couldn't have everything she wanted—nobody can. But he also quickly agreed when I told him this was falling on deaf ears. "You're right. The more I say, the less Jayne listens."

The reason for that, I told him, is that logic and reason seldom work. We all like to think of our kids as rational, and sometimes they are. But when it comes to listening to advice, using the toilet, brushing their teeth, or going to bed, a child's logic is that these are the very things that most often get in the way of what life is really about, which is having fun. They consider the parents who force these unwanted duties on them to be dumb, which is why she fights them tooth and nail.

The "expert" advice on dealing with out-of-control behavior is often so otherworldly that it sounds like a bad joke. The parents told me they had attended one program in which the instructor, a psychologist, actually suggested that when their offspring choose to go berserk, it is the parents, not the child, who should take the time-out. The premise of this gem was that the child isn't ready to be in control, and because that kind of behavior is just a natural phase of indeterminate duration, the best course for the parents is to find some quiet corner and patiently wait it out. But when the house is filled with screaming, smashing, and destructive rage, where might that quiet corner be? And the fact that the child has decided to forgo all civilized responsibility to the rest of the family hardly gives the parents a free pass to do likewise in return.

The paradox of this type of extreme behavior is that the out-of-control child is actually more in control than ever, at the center of the universe, forcing everyone within earshot into a reactive mode and establishing a single agenda for the whole family. Jayne's parents told me the books they read advised them to acknowledge the child's feelings, try to identify the problem behind the behavior, and then work with the screaming, flailing child to solve it. In other words, pretend the child is willing to be rational even though it is obvious the decision has been made to be wildly irrational. This rewards the behavior with undeserved attention and puts the inmate in charge of the asylum.

Help Wanted

When we went over the purpose of keeping the diary, the mother told me that they often praised Jayne but that now she realized it was for a relatively limited range of actions. They praised her for being smart; for using new words; for expressing herself clearly or, better yet, creatively; for being polite; for sharing with other kids; and for using the potty properly and in time. They had seldom praised her for taking disappointment calmly or for Mother Teresa behavior, because it hadn't occurred to them to pay much attention to that kind of interaction.

When we got to the part about reinforcing positive behavior with a vivid recollection of the event, the father told me they had been doing that in a limited way, but immediately rather than later. Also, instead of saying, "Good girl" or telling Jayne she had acted like a big girl, they usually said something like, "Good job." I told him this was not about their daughter's doing some kind of job—kids hate jobs. It was about Jayne.

The reason for Jayne's aggressive behavior toward her baby sister was resentment at the attention the sister got just for being a baby. Right after the sister was born, Jayne had started to regress—speaking in baby talk, paying less attention to getting on the potty, and spending more energy fighting her parents. This was because she reasoned that the baby got the attention in the family, and so she'd be a baby again. One of the lessons the parents had to teach her was that she could get a much better kind of attention by being more grown-up.

Over the next three weeks, using the diary and the ABCD techniques for positive reinforcement,

The paradox of this type of extreme behavior is that the out-of-control child is actually more in control than ever, at the center of the universe, forcing everyone within earshot into a reactive mode and establishing a single agenda for the whole family

Jayne's parents reported some results the mother described as "nothing short of a miracle." Among the diary notations in just the second week, Jayne went over to her sister's high chair and put her arms around her, kissed her, and told her she loved her. Later that same day she gave her favorite teddy bear to the sister to play with. She got her mother's shoes from under the kitchen table and brought them to her in the living room and then waited to see if she had any other errands for her. When told she couldn't eat a cookie just before supper, she put it back in the jar without a protest. When she started to play with a glass vase and her mother told her to stop, she immediately returned it to the corner shelf where she had found it.

Metamorphosis

Jayne is now 5, and her mother tells me the out-of-control behavior has vanished like a bad dream. She shares with her little sister, and instead of grabbing a toy to reclaim it, as she would have done before, she now asks, "Can I please have a turn?" Jayne started preschool this year, and on the first day, she asked if she could take her little sister with her. They walked the two blocks hand in hand, their delighted mother following a few paces behind.

Jayne's paternal grandmother told her daughter-in-law that the transformation was like watching a butterfly emerging from a cocoon. "You know it's inside, but until you actually see the result, it's hard to believe it can be so beautiful."

30

A CRIME AGAINST CHILDHOOD

⟨⟨∘——∘⟩⟩

BY NOW YOU PROBABLY recognize that most of the bad advice parents get for dealing with difficult children is interchangeable. What works for throwing, hitting, and biting also solves problems such as tantrums, screaming, jealousy, and not having any friends. *Let's talk about it. Rage is good. What are you really feeling? Tsk-tsk, sweetie pie, we try not to set fire to things.* One of the reasons for this replication is that all these behaviors tend to overlap, which is also why even the good advice can be a bit redundant. (What—you hadn't noticed?) But the Freudian approach to child raising owes its longevity to reasons all its own. In the absence of real science, and despite its wrong understanding of children's behavior and consistent disregard for the laws of learning, it has constructed a foundation of persistent, self-perpetuating myth.

The "Psychomythology Hall of Fame"

Because I so often have to deal with the consequences of those myths in the lives of the families I treat, I have drawn up a David Letterman–type list of the top ten contenders for the Psychomythology Hall of Fame. You've heard each of them in previous chapters, but here they are again all together, for one last look.

Myth #10 *It's a stage; he will outgrow it.*

Myth #9 *When kids misbehave, they need more love—"Children need love when they least deserve it."*

Myth #8 *When kids feel right, they will act right.*

Myth #7 *There are two types of tantrums: manipulative and temperamental.*

Myth #6 *Bad behavior is a symptom of emotional problems.*

Myth #5 *Psychobabble sounds smart, so it must mean something.*

Myth #4 *The temperament myth—"He can't help it; he was born that way."*

Myth #3 *Fake time-outs: talk, toys, and entertainment as "punishment."*

Myth #2 *Grin and bear it; misbehavior is an exciting preliminary to the next developmental stage.*

Myth #1 *The ultimate myth: the understanding myth, the need to get into the child's head and understand why he is misbehaving—"Don't get furious, get curious." Or, talk to the child as though you are a child.*

A theme common to most of these myths is the mistaken and illogical assumption that problem behaviors are an indication that the child is crying out for more quality time from the parent. This is totally false. The absurd extension of this fallacy is the notion that misbehavior by the child should always be answered by more love from the parent. If we all followed the trendy advice that "Children need love when they least deserve it," the guaranteed result would be more least-deserve-it behaviors.

The belief that behavior problems are simply a normal regression prior to the next exciting developmental stage is also nonsense. Parents who buy into the

> **A** theme common to most of these myths is the mistaken and illogical assumption that problem behaviors are an indication that the child is crying out for more quality time from the parent.

grin-and-bear-it myth and decide to hunker down until the child outgrows the Terrible Twos, for example, will find themselves waiting . . . and waiting . . . and waiting. Often they watch helplessly as the child passes through the even more terrible threes and then fours, fives, and sixes. The Terrible Twos are a fiction. As an explanation of misbehavior, developmental stages are nonexistent.

The myth about two types of tantrums—manipulative and temperamental—supports the absurd thesis that children who have tantrums actually can't help it. Experience proves just the opposite: virtually any child, regardless of circumstances or genetic legacy, can be taught impulse management and reliable self-control. A tantrum is a tantrum, and they are all alike in their purpose: to get what children want by driving parents nuts.

Psychobabble is the fanciful, extravagant, and largely meaningless language in which the parents of healthy children are given diagnoses for ordinary misbehaviors. Every one of the top ten myths has been constructed in support of just such a diagnosis. There is the spirited child, the explosive child, the difficult child, and the child with sensory integration disorder. Based on these and many other made-up diagnoses, parents are taught to play therapist, and the child becomes a patient. In the process, the parents are rewarding the exact behaviors that are driving them crazy—and making it that much harder for children to learn their way into growing up.

In the mythological time-out, the child and parent hold a running conversation on the steps, or the child is sent into a roomful of toys and games to reflect on his or her misdeeds. Talk and toys are rewards, not punishments, and they are almost never instructive or "therapeutic" as a response to misbehavior.

Which brings us to the most dangerous, dishonest, dastardly myth of all: that *any* childhood behaviors that make parenting more difficult or make teaching more challenging can be treated as a medical condition and eliminated by the use of drugs.

What If?

Consider the case histories in the preceding nine chapters.

Would tantrum-throwing Christie have turned into a better, happier, more promising high school junior if her tantrums when she was 5 had been treated with drugs instead of the kind of parental teaching that brought them to an end? And what are the life lessons she could possibly have learned from drugs?

What if Tommy's parents had chosen the all-too-frequently prescribed alternative to patient, methodical reinforcement? It's hard to imagine they would now be likely to boast that "Drugging him when he was 3 years old was 100 percent the key to changing Tommy's behavior." And what kind of behavior could we expect that to be?

When defiant Sam covered his ears and belted out songs to counter his parents' pleadings when he was 4, if someone had just popped a pill into his mouth to shut him up, how much better off would he be today? Certainly it would have saved his parents uncounted hours devoted to teaching him how to be a big boy and imparting the kinds of skills, knowledge, and self-control that will last a lifetime.

Maybe the really smart way to deal with Arthur every time he banged his 21-month-old head against the tray of his high chair would have been to force open his mouth and fill his head with brain drugs. Then watch him grow, if that's the word, from psychotropic boy to bionic man. Faster and cheaper, absolutely. But better?

It's uncertain whether Ritalin would have done much to improve Karen's problem in relating to other kids and keeping friends. More to the point, if her parents had elected that route when she was 6 instead of accepting their role as teachers, would she have any idea what she was missing? Would *anybody* know what she was missing?

After hitting his mother, biting his sister, and throwing objects at everyone in sight, what if little Burt had been drugged into compliance at the age of 2½, *Clockwork Orange*–style? Would he be more likely to become the prizefighter, baseball star, or champion bill collector his father had predicted? Or in a lifetime of incomplete growth and missed experiences, would he have to settle for hitting the pills?

Instead of parenting her little boy, if the mother of screaming Warren had allowed him to be drugged, what dreams do you suppose she would now be having?

Is there a pill for jealousy? You can bet your child's future on it. But if her parents had given that pill to Jenny Hogan, would they also be able to find her a pill for growing up?

And finally, there is out-of-control Jayne. What kind of butterfly would her parents be likely to see if they had decided to medicate instead of teach her? Without the learning, without the attention, without the struggle, and without the time it takes to grow up, would she have become a butterfly at all?

Bounty

The story I told you in Chapter 20 about the sheriff and the wanted posters is a lot more applicable to the practice of drugging than it is to

Not a single manufacturer of psychotropic drugs prescribed for "difficult" kids can guarantee the long-term effects of its products on the children's bodies or on their souls.

teaching. ADHD is a diagnosis without a disease. In several cases in which a particular drug was found to have a high correlation with childhood suicide or other forms of violence, the makers hid the results. Many drugs now prescribed for controlling difficult or disruptive children were FDA approved for some other application and *not for children*. Not a single manufacturer of psychotropic drugs prescribed for "difficult" kids can guarantee the long-term effects of its products on the children's bodies or on their souls. And not one of them offers a timetable for withdrawal. In fact, withdrawal isn't even on the manufacturers' agendas. Four of them fellers in jail? Three dead? Two still on the run? Holy smoke!

Compare that outcome with the story of the kids in Chapter 17 who had the fortitude to earn the second marshmallow. Super SATs. Goals for their future education and eventual careers that were over the horizon. Parents who taught them how to wait. Promising lives that have their roots in self-control. Wow!

Parents, you have the choice. Choose to teach your children, not to analyze them and not to buy into the big lies that lead to a made-up diagnosis. Above all, if you have any faith whatever in the future of our species, choose not to drug them.

Instead, choose life.

Epilogue

TOWARD A SCIENCE OF HUMAN BEHAVIOR

⟨•————•⟩

WHEN SIFTING THROUGH mountains of ash and dust in the aftermath of 9/11, forensic experts were able to isolate the remnants of the terrorists—a feat that would have been unimaginable less than a decade earlier. But the cellular fragments that proved their identities offered not a single clue as to why they did it.

The answers will not be found in the wreckage. Self-destructive fanaticism seems an illogical trait for genetic transmission. It is more reasonable to assume that it is not inherited but learned.

The same is true of most behavior, violent or otherwise. When a behavior becomes a social norm and is passed from one generation to the next, in almost every case the mechanism of transmission is environmental rather than genetic. Suicide bombers are the products of societal molding. So are rescuers, soldiers, and saints.

At the moment, we know far more about the building blocks of life than we do about the guidance system that determines how our lives are lived. The first is the subject of a newly emerging but already powerful science, while the other, though studied for millennia, still remains largely an art. Our knowledge of human behavior is as murky and incomplete as our understanding of the vast oceans. There has never been a more urgent need for a true science of human behavior.

There is a temptation to seek answers to behavior in the human genome, not only because the street is much better lit and there is now a map but because it's morally easier to reduce human character to a roll of the hereditary dice. The French naturalist Lamarck, an early evolutionist, raised a scientific sail with his insights into the architecture of natural structures, but at the same time he dropped an anchor with his belief in the inheritance of acquired characteristics. We now know that learned behavior leaves no imprint in the genes. Most of our faults and virtues are not in our stars but in what we have been taught. So in the one area where he is best remembered, Lamarck was dead wrong.

Sigmund Freud is now viewed by many behaviorists as the Lamarck of modern psychology: brilliant, innovative, and equally off the target. But the mental health profession as a whole is no more immune to the power of learned behavior than the rest of us, and this particular folly has proven to be unusually persistent. Despite a century of unmet promises, the industry is still so heavily invested in the mumbo-jumbo of ids and egos and superegos, most practitioners can't afford to take the write-off.

Pioneers are few and far between in any branch of knowledge, and massive change is always first perceived as heresy. To many of his peers, B. F. Skinner put his short-term reputation in a black box when he demonstrated how the principles governing human behavior are the same as those guiding the actions of our phylogenetic lessers. But he opened the door to a new era of understanding, as inviting, as mysterious, and as filled with rich promise as a door to the deep sea or outer space.

A true science of human behavior, if properly conceived and funded with the same level of commitment as we gave to the human genome, will yield more bounty than we can now imagine. It will hold the cure to diseases of our communal spirit—the dementia of war and terrorism, the cancer of selfishness and poverty, the Alzheimer's of apathy and forgetfulness of our own history—which threaten our lives, our civilization, our race, and our planet.

The need is urgent. The time is now.

Appendix A

THE INCREDIBLE GIFT
OF LEARNING

❦

*Several years ago I was asked to contribute a chapter on learning for a professional textbook on psychology (*Contemporary Issues in Behavior Therapy: Improving the Human Condition *[New York: Plenum Press, 1996]). It is offered here, in abridged form, for parents who are interested in gaining a better understanding of how learning happens.*

TWO ESSENTIAL GOALS for humans are survival of the individual and survival of the species. Consequently, within the genetic structure of humans, eating behavior, and therefore survival of the individual, was guaranteed by way of food's being a powerful reinforcer. Likewise within the genetic structure, survival of the species was guaranteed by making sexual behavior a powerful reinforcer. The result is that 6.5 billion people now occupy this small planet Earth.

201

For other species, instinct is a major part of the genetic makeup. The ant and bee, for instance, generally behave in fixed ways because their behavior is governed by their genes. Humans, however, have been given a precious gift, the gift of learning. This gift of learning, in combination with a powerful brain, enables us to take charge of our world. We have learned to fly like the birds at rates that exceed the speed of sound, to send color pictures around the globe and beyond, and to escape the bonds of gravity and travel to the moon and back safely; we have built impressive structures, discovered cures for threatening diseases, and learned how to alter our own genetic makeup and thereby correct genetic defects. We are able to do all of this because we live in a universe that is orderly. Day will follow night, summer will follow spring, and comets will travel the universe and make their rounds in an orderly manner with precision.

The combination of brainpower, lawfulness within the universe, and this incredible gift of learning enables humans to work to achieve what Thomas Jefferson said was the God-given right to life, liberty, and the pursuit of happiness. However, in addition to laws of physics and biology, there must be laws of behavior.

Us Versus Them

B. F. Skinner viewed human behavior as learned, governed not by inner and unseen causes but by the consequences that follow the behavior. On the other hand, Eda Le Shan views human behavior in a radically different way:

> I do not agree with the new breed of psychologists who are telling parents that there are formulas for child raising. These psychologists, called behaviorists, have their roots back with Pavlov and his salivating dogs. They

believe in conditioning, that people can be made to behave in certain ways by conditioned responses. They are right about white rats; it works very well on them. It also works on people for short periods of time. But to my relief and delight, conditioning (which is learning) does not have lasting effects, and sooner or later the marvelous unpredictability of human beings comes through again.

The ridicule of Skinner's understanding of human behavior is not dissimilar from ridicule that others before him experienced when they denied humans a feeling of being unique and special.

As humans, we find it difficult to accept the fact that in this vast universe we are not special. Charles Darwin, in his theory of evolution, stated that biologically we are not unique beings created in the image of the Almighty. Though Darwin was not subjected to house arrest as was Galileo, his thinking was met with equal, if not greater, resistance.

Today a man of equal stature, B. F. Skinner, the late professor of psychology at Harvard University, is being subjected to the same fate as Galileo and Darwin. Galileo said we are not special within the universe, not at its center. Darwin said we are not special biologically. And Skinner said we are not special behaviorally.

For far too long, the field of psychiatry has set the tone of our understanding of ourselves, for reasons that have little to do with the worth of its therapeutic procedures. The profession of psychiatry has made us feel special for a hundred years by operating totally apart from the scientific method, with a theory so vague, so lacking in precision, that it is virtually untestable. Its practitioners have, however, more than made up for their lack of therapeutic methodology with techniques of persuasion that are without equal. The profession of psychiatry (Freud's "talking cure") is much like the emperor with no clothing. The time has come for the public to view the emperor's garb for what it truly is.

A mother nursing her child gives of herself, her milk, to nurture this tiny being. While we never question the need to nurture the child's physical being, there is a form of nurture that is equally important by way of warmth, love, and physical contact. Experiments on monkeys clearly indicate that the physical contact between mother and infant is crucial in determining future development. The absence of physical contact creates serious negative developmental consequences.

The fact that infants need this physical contact and warmth above and beyond nurture to meet their psychological needs was also clearly demonstrated in the maternal deprivation studies of Rene Spitz. Spitz studied two groups of children born to women prisoners. The conditions of the groups differed, he said, "in one single factor—the amount of emotional interchange offered." In one institution, the children were raised by their mothers. In the second institution, they were raised from the third month by overworked nursing personnel; one nurse had to care for from eight to twelve children.

Spitz found that the group raised by their mothers did better by all standards of development. They were healthier, had a lower mortality rate, grew faster, were better adjusted, and were happier than the babies in the foundling home. The most striking finding was the mortality rate. In the group that stayed with their mothers, there were no deaths during the two-year period of the study, whereas in the foundling home 37 percent of the infants died. Spitz, who used the term *marasmus* to describe this situation, reported: "The high mortality is but the most extreme consequence of the general decline, both physical and psychological, which is shown by children completely starved of emotional interchange."

Clearly, the mother's milk of children's behavior is love, warmth, and physical contact. "He (or she) is doing it for attention" is the repeated explanation of why children misbehave. It may sound trite, but it is so true. "He is eating because he is hungry" is also a truism.

Children who misbehave for attention are not necessarily hungry for human contact. Usually they are not attention deprived. More often than not, they are simply behaving in this way because it is immediately effective in bringing human contact, much like the overweight person who eats to excess because it is immediately satisfying. Often children who misbehave the most are getting an abundance of attention and human contact and are not attention deprived, just as the overweight person is not food deprived.

The mother's milk of behavior is attention and love, but we must look upon this milk as being of varying quality. Though the ultimate reinforcing consequences for children's behavior is human contact, this contact runs along a continuum from love, warmth, touching, and praise at one end, to simple attention on the other end. Human contact is so powerful a reinforcing consequence for the child that it will nurture behavior even at the lowest quality levels. Yelling, screaming, and anger from a person called mother or father is a potent reinforcing consequence and often is referred to as negative attention.

The First Behavior Therapist

Annie Sullivan, Helen Keller's teacher, was labeled a "miracle worker" and is widely accepted as such. Not so obvious to most people, however, is the fact that in reality Annie Sullivan was the first known behavior therapist. She was the first individual on record to systematically apply the laws of human behavior to helping a hurt human being—in this case, someone who went on to remarkable achievements. Helen Keller, blind and deaf nearly from birth, was in every sense a human being with vast potential. Her potential lay untapped because she was being given love for the wrong behaviors. The following conversation from William Gibson's play *The Miracle Worker* illustrates this state of affairs:

KATE (HELEN KELLER'S MOTHER): You know she began talking when she was 6 months old? She could say "water." I never saw a child so bright or outgoing. It's still in her, somewhere, isn't it? You should have seen her before her illness, such a good-tempered child.

ANNIE SULLIVAN: She's changed.

KATE: Miss Annie, put up with it. And with us. Please? Like the lost lamb in the parable, I love her all the more.

ANNIE: Mrs. Keller, I don't think Helen's worst handicap is deafness or blindness. I think it's your love. And pity. All of us here are so sorry for her. You've kept her—like a pet; why, even a dog you housebreak. No wonder she won't let me come near her. It's useless for me to try to teach her language or anything else here.

Fortunately for Helen Keller—and for the rest of the world—this was not the final conversation Annie Sullivan was to have in the Keller household. She remained, worked hard, and eventually changed the way Helen's family treated her—and therefore changed the way Helen learned behaviors. What Helen Keller's family was doing was giving a destructive form of love: pity. She was receiving love for the wrong behaviors, love when she least deserved it.

The Incredible Gift of Learning

What I find fascinating about human behavior is its variability. This variability springs from the gift of learning. Most of us think of learning in terms of the three Rs, but learning begins long before the time of formal schooling. Children's first teachers are their parents.

We must look upon children's behavior in a new way, one so simple that it is radical. The best way to understand the gift of learning in children is through a garden analogy. In a garden you have both valued plants and weeds. The role of the parent is to nurture the valued plants and eliminate the weeds.

How does the child learn? How do parents teach? These are essential questions. It is unfortunate that we often overlook the extreme importance of early learning experiences, and for the most part these extremely important teachers called parents teach by the seat of their pants. Though we are becoming increasingly aware of the necessity of providing children with good nutrition, our understanding of the value of nurturing behaviors is at a relatively primitive level.

On the Nurturing of Behavior

Until just recently we seldom looked at behavior as a subject in and of itself. We were so fascinated by the alleged inner workings of the "mind" that we overlooked what was right before our eyes: behavior.

Sigmund Freud made the workings of the unconscious a compelling realm of study. It was, and unfortunately still is, to most people far more provocative than behavior itself. His influence is a major contributor to our inclination to look within rather than at behavior and environmental consequences.

The workings of this fiction called the mind fascinate those who are the most intelligent because such people obtain their reinforcing satisfactions by way of endlessly putting the pieces of the personality puzzle together. The most intelligent people confuse behavior "understanding" with behavior control. They are so fascinated by the process of putting the pieces of their personality puzzle together that they overlook the fact that what really matters is behavior change and an improved quality of life. The idea that understanding will set you free is a fiction. For adults this fiction is carried out by professionals using what Freud called the "talking cure," and for children it's through play therapy.

But do insight and understanding change behavior? Does what Freud said about making the unconscious conscious change behavior? The answer is no. Studies going to the very source of the theory, Freud's own cases, indicate that this theory was flawed from the outset. Frank Sulloway, a historian of science at the Massachusetts Institute of Technology, reviewed the cases that Freud reported as his major successes and found that they were in fact total failures. Freud was an excellent writer who distorted the facts to fit his theory. Insight does not produce behavior change:

> Freud published only six detailed case histories after he broke with Breuer and developed the "talking cure" into psychoanalysis proper. Examined critically, these six case histories are by no means compelling empirical demonstrations of the correctness of his psychoanalytical views. Indeed, some of the cases present such dubious evidence in favor of psychoanalytic theory that one may seriously wonder why Freud even bothered to publish them. As Seymour Fisher and Roger Greenberg have commented in connection with their own review of the case histories, "It is curious and striking that Freud chose to demonstrate the utility of psychoanalysis through descriptions of largely unsuccessful cases."

And hence a demonstration of Freud's brilliant analytic powers. Sulloway goes on to say:

> Of course, the fact that the Wolf Man, Anna O., and various other famous psychoanalytic patients were not cured is not technically a refutation of Freud's clinical theories and claims. These cases *can* be admitted as failures, or as only partial successes, and Freud's theories could still

be correct. But research since the 1930s has shown repeatedly that psychoanalytic patients fare no better than patients who participate in more than a hundred other forms of psychotherapy. Freud maintained on the contrary that psychoanalysis was the only form of psychotherapy that could produce true and permanent cures—all other therapeutic successes being due to suggestion. As Hans Eysenck [a renowned research psychologist] has argued, the failure of psychoanalysis to achieve *superior* cure rates, as promised, should be taken as strong evidence of its theoretical failure.

A new round of historical research on Sigmund Freud is challenging the reputation of the founder of psychoanalysis. New revelations depict a Freud who seems at times mercenary and manipulative, who sometimes claimed cures where there were none and who on occasion distorted the facts of his cases to prove his theoretical points.

The most startling discoveries, many not yet published, concern some of Freud's most important cases, including the patients he referred to as Little Hans and Dora. As Sulloway stated, "Each of Freud's published cases plays a role in the psychoanalytic legend. The more detail you learn about each case, the stronger the image becomes of Freud twisting the facts to fit his theory." The new historical work is just the kind of inquiry that Freud dreaded. He burned many of his papers at different points in his life and destroyed most of his case notes.

The belief that insight has curative powers and will change behaviors is based on the medical or disease model of behavior. Mental health professionals often refer to problem behaviors as symptoms or as symptomatic of some inner, intrapsychic disease process called emotional problems.

Why is this way of understanding human behavior false for behavior but true for diseases that affect the physiology of the human organ-

ism? The answer was best stated in the book *Getting the Love You Want.*
The author, Harville Hendrix, explains why insight is not enough and
is only a small step in the process of behavior and feeling change:

> Years ago I was resistant to the idea of such a direct approach to the alter-
> ation of my client's behavior. Coming from a psychoanalytic tradition, I
> was taught that the goal of the therapist was to help the clients remove
> their emotional blocks. Once they had correctly linked feelings they had
> about their partners with needs and desires left over from childhood, they
> were supposed automatically to evolve to a more rational, adult style of
> relating. This assumption was based on the medical model that, once a
> physician cures a disease, the patient automatically returns to full health.
> Since most forms of psychotherapy come from psychoanalysis, which, in
> turn, has its roots in nineteenth-century medicine, the fact that they rest
> on a common biological assumption is not surprising. But years of expe-
> rience with couples convinced me that a medical model is not a useful one
> for marital therapy. When a physician cures a disease, the body recovers
> spontaneously because it relies on genetic programming. Each cell of the
> body, unless it is damaged or diseased, contains all the information it needs
> to function normally. But there is no genetic code that governs marriage
> (or children's behavior). Marriage (or children's behavior) is a cultural cre-
> ation *imposed* on biology. Because people lack a built-in set of social
> instructions, they can be trapped in unhappy relationships after months
> or even years of productive therapy. Their emotional blocks may be
> removed, and they may have insight into the cause of their difficulties, but
> they still cling to habituated behaviors.

A Garden of Behaviors

Years ago when I would visit my parents at their retirement home in
Florida, I would wonder at the large tree in their front yard, which I

recognized as a schefflera (more commonly known as an umbrella tree). It was more than forty feet high and had a trunk one and a half feet in diameter. Was this the same type of tree, I wondered, that I would often see up north in a supermarket that sold ornamental plants? It was in fact the same. Where I lived, it was only six feet high, and the diameter of its trunk was no more than an inch. The same combination of genes in one environment grew to a height in excess of forty feet and in another environment produced a much smaller plant. The phenomenon is similar to that of the tree on the top of a mountain that is stunted in growth, versus the same tree at ground level that grows to its full potential.

The same principles apply to children's behavior. What can parents do to provide for their child's behavior what might be termed a "Florida environment"—enabling the child, by way of a nurturing environment, to more closely achieve his or her genetic potential?

I visualized a garden of behaviors in which parents supply maximum nourishment for their children's behavioral and feeling growth. Behaviors, like seedlings in a garden, need to be nourished, and that nourishment is provided by consequences. Parents must also be taught how not to encourage weeds. There are many weeds in this garden. In fact, parents have been prompted to nurture weeds by members of my own profession. I once walked into a child guidance clinic and saw on the wall a sign professing "Children Need Love When They Least Deserve It." Without a doubt, if you follow this dictum, you will be nurturing weeds.

Helen Keller during her early years, before Annie Sullivan came on the scene, was a child whose parents felt sorry for her because she was blind and deaf. They nurtured the weeds and in the process created a monster. Annie Sullivan was the first behavior therapist and helped Helen Keller fulfill her God-given genetic potential by eliminating the weeds and nurturing the behaviors that led her to become a woman of great achievement.

The Seeds

Children during their early years are "all eyes and ears." As a matter of course, they want to learn, and what they learn is what they hear and see within their environment. The seeds are provided, by and large, by parents. The seeds of verbal behavior are everywhere and are an integral part of the child's environment. Parents seldom need training to nurture verbal behaviors, and almost without exception they give their love, warmth, and praise for every new word that the child imitates— *mama, dada, ball, cookie*. The result is that children learn their native tongue with ease, even though this involves mastering a complex set of behaviors. Some children never stop talking, and that's simply because of the incredible power of the consequences of praise, warmth, and love immediately following imitated verbal behaviors.

Verbal behaviors as a matter of course are always given a Florida environment. But there are other behaviors that parents often do not see. These behaviors are critical to the child's growth and development and are the foundation of feelings of self-esteem and achievement, both social and academic. Parents seldom see these behaviors because they are drowned out by behaviors that are "noisy" or have been labeled as symptoms of emotional problems. We have been taught to analyze the weeds in the garden, and in the process we overlook what is most important—those delicate, quiet seedling behaviors that are the foundation of success, happiness, and self-worth.

Parents must ask themselves, What do I want to teach and encourage in this garden of behaviors? In general, parents want their children to be independent and mature, to become successful, and to feel a sense of self-worth and fulfillment as adults. Parents want their children to be successful later in life in what Freud spoke of as the two most important aspects of living, "Lieben und arbeiten"—love and work. But success in love and work requires those quiet behaviors that we so seldom see.

These behaviors, like the delicate seedlings in a garden, are in many cases destroyed by the abundance of weed growth that often is encouraged by way of talk and play therapies in and out of the therapists' office.

Here are the most-prized seedlings—the categories of behaviors that must be nurtured:

1. Speaking—as discussed earlier
2. Taking disappointment calmly (the opposite of tantrums when things do not go one's way)
3. Sibling caring (the opposite of sibling rivalry)
4. Mother Teresa behaviors (thinking of the other person—the opposite of self-centered behaviors)
5. Thirst for learning
6. Friendship and social skills

These categories of behaviors have one thing in common: the related behaviors all reflect increasing maturity and steps toward adulthood. With few exceptions, children want to be more like adults; in fact, being called a "big boy" or a "big girl" is a powerful consequence.

The Primacy of Early Learning

There is increasing evidence that the early years are a critical period for learning behavior, which underscores the extreme importance of learning in early childhood. Recent studies on brain function during these early years indicate that learning is facilitated in the young child by the abundance of nerve cell connections during this period. Here's a synopsis:

1. In the first year of life, the infant's brain doubles in weight, and nerve cells sprout branches that connect with other branches, with the

number snowballing from 50 trillion to 1,000 trillion. This exuberance of connections is part of nature's design to build bridges between nerve cells so that learning is possible.

2. Nerve cells put many more connections into place than they intend to retain. What determines the survival of connections is the experience of the organism.

3. Each and every experience—each sight, each noise, each hug—strengthens specific nerve cell connections in the brain. Some connections get stronger and survive, while some get weaker and wilt away. Scientists revert to a gardening term to describe this thinning out of nerve cell connections: they call it pruning.

4. Most of this sculpting takes place within the first decade of life. At the level of each nerve cell connection, the name of the game is "use it or lose it."

5. If you are brought up in a family in which music is particularly valued and everybody's a musician, well then, certainly those are kinds of connections that tend to be strongly stabilized. Likewise, if you are a baby in a family in which several languages are spoken, the nerve cell connections that decipher the sounds of language are constantly being activated.

Maladaptation

There is no doubt that many adult maladaptive behaviors are ones learned in childhood. They are adaptive at that time and continue throughout adulthood in spite of the fact that the environment has markedly changed. In studies, rats deprived of food during the first weeks of their existence engage in hoarding behavior for life, though they are thereafter given food in abundance. Similarly, adults who were children during the Depression years may behave in ways that reflect maladaptive behavior patterns in spite of a radically changed adult environment. Do we really need an unconscious to explain what appears to be irrational behavior patterns? It is nothing more than learning, pure and simple.

Those Seedling Behaviors

The seedlings are imitated behaviors. The positive, quiet seedling behaviors need more than praise. Five to ten seconds of praise can in no way compete with the many minutes and hours parents often give contingent on negative seedling behaviors—the weeds. Parents must learn methods to nurture these quiet seedling behaviors that so often go unremarked. There are two basic classes of positive seedling behaviors:

1. Mother Teresa behaviors: Any behavior that indicates that the child is other-person-centered rather than self-centered. A subcategory is sibling caring behavior, a behavior that needs to be nurtured as a first step toward eliminating sibling rivalry.

2. Taking disappointment calmly: Any behavior indicating that the child has experienced a situation that did not go his or her way and the response was relatively calm and accepting. This is what children who have tantrums need to learn and is the opposite of temper tantrum behavior.

It is noteworthy that these classes of behavior have never been highlighted by behavioral psychologists and yet are crucial to child development.

Children as part of growing up must of necessity learn to handle disappointment and also to be sensitive to the needs, wishes, and feelings of others who live with them on this planet. Mother Teresa behavior is what Dr. Richard Stuart (1980) talks about when he teaches couples to show caring in his marital counseling method called "caring days." Caring for others—a sensitivity to the needs, feelings, and wishes of other people—is essential in all human relationships and is an indication that the child is mature, more other-person-oriented than self-centered. Taking disappointment calmly is also an indication of increasing maturity.

If we are ever to improve the human condition, it will be necessary to understand those learning experiences during the formative years of a child's life. For more than a hundred years, children's behavior has been viewed not as the fruit of learning but as the product of deep-rooted unconscious conflicts within the psyche.

If we are to make progress in achieving our inalienable right to the pursuit of happiness, we must begin to look at behavior in a new way: not as the result of unseen inner events but as the result of consequences. The cause follows the behavior.

Appendix B

FEEDBACK

⟪◦———◦⟫

Comments from Physicians

I have sent many families to Dr. Azerrad. His input has been very helpful. I saw one of these families recently. Several years ago they were having a difficult time with their now 7-year-old son. He has become a delight. I asked what factor played the biggest role in bringing about this change. Without a pause, the mother said, "Dr. Azerrad."

—Ron Schneebaum, M.D.

I am highly recommending Dr. Azerrad, a well-known clinical psychologist in Lexington, Massachusetts. I have referred patients to him for the past ten years. These cases are usually of the most difficult type, consisting of parents having children with severe behavioral problems. He works wonders for these troubled families where others have failed to help. I again highly advise using Dr. Azerrad as a solid asset in your referral system.

—GARY L. GOLDFARB, M.D.

As a practicing pediatrician in the Boston area, I have had numerous occasions to need referral help in behavioral and psychological problems with children. I have had parents and children report excellent results with Dr. Azerrad. I have been especially pleased with parents of children with obsessive behaviors or family dysfunction. His very practical approach has been very reassuring and successful with many families I have sent to him.

—CHARLES S. BROWN, M.D.

And from Parents

Patient #1: A Family at Crisis Point

We are the parents of a difficult-to-handle 4-year-old boy who was seriously disrupting our home life with destructive, impulsive, and aggressive behavior. We came to the realization that we were incapable of dealing with our son, so we sought professional help. Our HMO gave us a list of psychologists, from which we chose one in Salem, Massachusetts. Our family was at a crisis point. Our son was totally unmanageable. He was having temper tantrums that would lead to the deliberate destruction of our property. He would physically attack our other two children, then ages 9 months and 8, leaving them crying, bruised, and sometimes bleeding. Children outside of our home would not play with him because he would attack them by throwing rocks, hitting them with anything he could lift—an umbrella, toys, sticks, a baseball bat, etc. He would run into them with his bike and call them names. We avoided visiting relatives and friends because we were afraid he would deliberately break something, hurt other children, or otherwise humiliate or embarrass us with his outrageous behavior.

The HMO approved our request for mental health benefits, twenty visits per calendar year per family member, and we began therapy. We saw the Salem doctor one hour per week for the next five months: half an hour for family counseling and the other half hour individual counseling for our son. During the five months, we were also referred to a psychometrician, a psychiatrist, and a neurologist. We were advised to begin a program of rewards for our little boy: when he did something "good," we were to put a star on a chart, and we were to subtract a star when he was "bad." This system worked well—for about a week. Then we tried another. In this next attempt, he was encouraged to behave for five-minute intervals through the use of an egg timer. It also worked well—for about three days. End of helpful hints from the psychologist. The remainder of our visits was spent rehashing the prior week's events, and *our* childhoods, *our* relationships with *our* parents. We were made to feel extremely guilty, inadequate, and totally without affection for our son. As for our son, the psychologist was "trying to build a relationship with him" while *our* relationship with each other, our son, and our other two children continued on a downhill course.

By late October we were still no closer to a solution to our problems, and as our boy's mother, I could not deal with all the guilt that was being thrust upon me. Eventually, at the urging of my parents, I spoke to my family doctor of my feelings of desperation and depression, and he prescribed medication to help me cope with our situation. He finally agreed that we should stop seeing the psychologist because we were not progressing as we felt we should. We terminated our therapy despite the fact that we had already applied for additional mental health benefits and were approved. We were again in a time of crisis. The behaviors that brought us into therapy had only become worse. Once again we were desperate to find someone who could help.

We then heard about Dr. Jacob Azerrad and his unique approach to dealing with difficult children. Without his ever seeing our son, he could teach us his techniques, and we would see improvement within three weeks. Our first visit was encouraging. In the first step to achieving what we then considered to be an impossible goal, we were told to observe and record as many mature, responsible, independent behaviors in our child as possible. At the end of the first week, we were amazed at the number of mature behaviors. We had been concentrating so much on his negative behavior that the positive behaviors went unnoticed.

At our second visit we were taught how to praise these mature behaviors (step two). No more than four to five times that week, we were to make note of a mature behavior that we could praise from one hour to six hours later. Privately, we would re-create the behavior with a vivid description, give "100 percent praise" to him for the behavior, tell him why the behavior was valued, and, almost as an afterthought, suggest we do something that he likes to do (five to ten minutes only), as a way of reinforcing the behavior.

At our third visit we discussed punishment for those behaviors that were injurious to our son or other people (step three). These "target behaviors" would be discouraged by a "time-out" system in which he would be given as *little* attention as possible for inappropriate behaviors. It must be done so precisely that we spoke by phone to Dr. Azerrad for the first three days we used it to be sure we were doing it correctly. We have also continued recording and praising mature behaviors.

At our fourth visit we had nothing but optimism for our son's future and ours. Today he is visibly happier than we have ever seen him. He smiles most of the time! He is learning to control his own behavior; he can stop himself from hitting about 40 percent of the time. Now he is learning to compromise, handle disappointment, play with other children, care for the feelings of other people, help with household chores, and take more responsibility for himself. This means such things as washing well, dressing for the weather, pouring himself something to drink, taking care of his clothes, hanging up his coat, and finding his own shoes. He is also learning that he can be close to us by acting mature and responsible instead of being disruptive.

Because he is only 4 years old, he cannot change his behavior without our changing the environment in which he misbehaves. Dr. Azerrad has helped us, with his commonsense approach to child rearing, to effectively begin to change this environment. The best news of all is that Dr. Azerrad feels that we will need only two or three additional visits in order to continue forward progress. Our only regret is that we wasted so much time and money in conventional therapy. In only four weeks the atmosphere in our home has been completely transformed; our unhappy and disruptive child of four weeks ago is learning to be cooperative and caring—and happier.

Patient #2: Nothing to Lose

I am the mother of an 8-year-old girl. Approximately one year ago my daughter began behaving in a negative, angry, confrontational manner. We couldn't get through a day without fighting, and our family life began to deteriorate. It was tense and volatile, with hollering, crying, threats, and withholding of privileges. Nothing was working. It became so intolerable that I shuddered in the morning hearing my daughter's voice as she woke, thinking of how soon we would be at one another— the angry words and bad feelings. This was affecting my other daughter as well.

Because nothing I was doing—talking, spending extra time together, ignoring the behavior, and so on—was working, I started asking people for advice. Dr. Azerrad was recommended, and it was probably the best recommendation I have ever got. I visited his office with much skepticism and with an air of desperation and a "show me" attitude. I felt that I'd failed as a mother and that my relationship with her had got to the point where it could not be turned around.

Why my daughter behaved as she did is irrelevant. The fact is that the techniques and the approach mapped out for me and my daughter worked. They worked in a very short period of time. I think we had perhaps ten consultations with Dr. Azerrad. During that time I learned to observe my daughter's mature, positive behaviors and to comment positively and vividly, re-creating with words those things she did that I considered mature and positive. I learned that no matter how insignificant they seemed, it was worthwhile to make mention of them to my child. At first it all felt terribly artificial and contrived, but I did feel I had nothing to lose and everything to gain. And gain I did. My daughter slowly became a true delight to be with! My attitude toward her began to change. In a matter of a few weeks, "as if by magic," my feelings and behavior toward my child were ten times more loving. We began to joke and laugh together. We started to hug one another again. Most important, I learned that I could, as Dr. Azerrad put it, love my child not for what she did, not for her behaviors, but just for herself.

I still find myself automatically falling into the steps I learned. I use the techniques automatically, praising any mature, positive behaviors, no matter how small. I don't take those behaviors for granted. I don't expect mature behavior all the time, but my girls know they'll hear some good words from their mom when they do react maturely. And they still puff up with self-pleasure even if they've heard a thousand times how pleased I am.

My family has turned around; my home and my daughters are a source of infinite pleasure to me. Last year at this time, I would not have believed it. Bravo, Dr. Azerrad!

Patient #3: Valium Isn't the Answer

The reason we came to see Dr. Azerrad was ongoing behavioral problems with our oldest child, a 7-year-old boy. More than four years ago, my husband and I became aware of increased aggressive behavior. At that time, when our son was only 3, it was directed primarily at me, his mother. Since then the aggression, physical and verbal, grew to include his father, sister, and friends.

We have seen two psychiatrists and two psychologists since this began. One psychiatrist suggested I take Valium to help me deal with it. (We didn't return.) Although the sessions prior to seeing Dr. Azerrad helped me cope with the frustration and allowed my husband and me a way of dealing with the problems, the aggressive behavior continued at home. However, it was not a problem at school or at other homes.

Our son was seen on a regular weekly basis for approximately one year by a psychologist, with occasional family meetings. Although there was periodic improvement, it was not lasting. The psychologist was the one who referred us to Dr. Azerrad, as he was unable to get to "the root of the matter." I do feel that the psychologist helped our son in a way, as a stabilizing factor. When the visits with him decreased, the negative behaviors worsened.

We have been seeing Dr. Azerrad weekly for the past three months to find ways to teach our son appropriate behaviors. During that time, our son has seen Dr. Azerrad only twice. We have accomplished more in those ninety days than in the prior three years. We still have a long way to go, but slowly our son is learning positive, acceptable behaviors, such as being a caring person, good friend, and good brother and handling disappointment in stride. It is a vast improvement to see him walk away from a situation with his sister instead of punching her in the stomach. By working with an "I am proud" notebook, credit system, and positive praise, there is a way of dealing with negative behaviors without seeing the child in weekly sessions.

There are still times when I get discouraged with the amount of effort it takes to redirect these behaviors; it is definitely not an overnight success, but it can work. As Dr. Azerrad has explained to us, these new positive behaviors are fragile; we have many years of negative to undo. My husband and I know that inside our child is a loving and caring person emerging. Any amount of time devoted to that kind of cause is worth it.

Patient #4: Mistress Mary

Our daughter had tantrums two or three times a day, yelling, screaming, and slamming doors. Any frustration would trigger it. She would throw a fit if she didn't get her way, if I told her to do something, if I did something for her that she decided she wanted done in a different way, or if she had to wait for me to finish something before I gave her what she wanted. She was contrary for the sake of being contrary. She would act out by hitting her brother, flailing her arms, cursing, pushing the table at dinner—anything to get attention.

After seeing Dr. Azerrad, I began with the positive comments and reinforcement. If she did something like helping to put away garbage cans, I would say, "That is big girl behavior. I'm so proud of you." Later I would take her aside and remind her of what she did, again tell her how proud I was of her, and say why I liked what she did—because it showed that she cared and wanted to help me—and then I always asked her if she wanted to hear a story.

I reinforce any positive behavior, anything she does. It may not necessarily be on our list, but I comment on and praise *anything* she does that shows patience, maturity, and consideration. She has said, "I'm so glad you are my mommy" about five times in the last four days. We are at the beginning of the end with her tantrums. There was a hint of one the other morning when she took off her coat and announced she didn't want to go to school, but when I helped her put it back on, she continued on her way. She seems much happier—no acting out and nicer to her brother, father, and me.

Patient #5: Doctors Aren't Immune: Geraldine Cassens, Ph.D., Director of Neuropsychology, The Institute of Living

I consulted with Dr. Azerrad because of behavioral difficulties experienced by my daughter, then 5. I told him she was having erratic tantrums and bed-wetting seven nights per week, up to three times per night. I was referred to him by both a physician and a friend whose child had a similar problem.

Using behavioral techniques and a schedule of observation and reinforcement, within a period of a few weeks he transformed these behavioral difficulties with my daughter into nonexistence. His professional manner was expedient, methodical, positive, and based on professional practices in behavior modification. While I theoretically knew behavioral techniques were effective and maximized gain in efficiency (I had taught courses in behavioral theory myself), I was amazed at how quickly his suggestions and therapy guides turned my ineffective and erratic behavioral practices into careful, positive, and rewarding ones.

I have been so pleased with his professional care that I have referred him to many of my colleagues and friends. In addition, since I am a practicing neuropsychologist, I have referred clients to Dr. Azerrad for behavior therapy. I must add that one of the reasons I sought Dr. Azerrad for therapy for my daughter was that he was able to change her behavior through guidelines and suggestions for *my* behavior. I think this is particularly appropriate in young children for whom insight therapy and long-term psychotherapy are inappropriate.

Patient #6: From "Go Away" to "Play with Me"

Our child is now cooperative; he shares; he has manners; he says, "Thank you" and "You're welcome." When I ask him to help me out, he does it and says proudly, "I'm Mom's helper guy." Before, he would do everything he could to run away from me; now he takes my hand when we cross the street. He used to say, "Go away" all the time; now he says, "I want Mommy to stay with me" or "Play with me." He says, "Thank you" to kids without my asking him to if we go to a neighbor's house to play, and if they use the neighbor's toys, he says, "Thank you for letting me play with your toys." Before, whenever I would tell him it was time to go, he would have a complete breakdown; I'd have to pick him up and carry him out.

What are the reasons for these changes? Mother Teresa, ABCD, and perhaps most of all, my giving him positive reinforcement. He sees that I am noticing what he is doing. He sees that I am remembering. He loves when I take him aside to give him time. He smiles and puts his arms around my neck.

Patient #7: Les Miserables

The specific event that led to our coming to Dr. Azerrad was when the family went to York Beach and she had a meltdown in the park because she couldn't go on a certain ride with somebody. She was always whiny, not happy; everything was a problem, and it was spilling over to her sisters and her friends. She didn't seem to be getting along with anyone. Her older sister, who lets things roll off her back, was becoming annoyed and didn't want to be around her. Other kids didn't want to be near her, for the same reasons. If she didn't get her own way, she would make the situation miserable for everybody—and that was most of the time.

Two months later: she is delightful, nice to be around, and polite; she listens; she tries to help when she can; she is kind to her sisters; and most of all, she is happy. She has stopped whining, which is a huge thing. Everything was a whine. She is different. We went with her to the guidance counselor and teacher, and they thought she was a completely different child from last year.

What were the reasons for the change? I stopped focusing on all her negative behavior that was driving me up the wall and now am concentrating on her positive behavior. I am focusing on her stopping the whining, being a good friend, listening, Mother Teresa behaviors, sibling caring behaviors, and friend behaviors.

Patient #8: Praise for Praise

The incentive plan for reinforcing big boy behaviors was the most helpful recommendation. I wasn't sure how well it would work, but with lots of praise, it works wonderfully and wasn't difficult to phase out either. I use it now only if and when an occasion arises.

Patient #9: Thanks All Around

John has learned self-control and exercises it. The ABCD method was helpful, and so was the time-out method. You helped us through a difficult time and learning process. We all thank you.

REFERENCES

Azerrad, J. (1980). *Anyone Can Have a Happy Child.* New York: M. Evans.

Cautela, J. R. (1970). "Covert Reinforcement," *Behavior Therapy*, 1: 33–50.

Ellis, A. (1990). Live at the Learning Annex. (Public discussion.) New York.

Freud, S. (1916). *Introductory Lectures on Psychoanalysis*, Vol. 16. New York: Liveright.

Gibson, W. (1957). *The Miracle Worker.* New York: Knopf.

Harlow, H. F., and R. R. Zimmerman (1959). "Affectional Response in the Infant Monkey," *Science*, 130: 431–432.

Hendrix, H. (1990). *Getting the Love You Want.* New York: Perennial Library.

Le Shan, E. (1965). *How to Survive Parenthood.* New York: Random House.

National Public Radio (1994, October 4). "All Things Considered" (radio broadcast). Oct. 4. Washington, DC: Author.

New York Times (1983). "Galileo 'Heresies' Still Under Study, Pope Says." May 10, p. A12.

Skinner, B. F. (1953). *Science and Human Behavior.* New York: Free Press.

——— (1971). *Beyond Freedom and Dignity.* New York: Knopf.

Spitz, R. A. (1949). "Motherless Infants," *Child Development*, 20: 145–155.

Stuart, R. B. (1980). *Helping Couples Change.* New York: Guilford Press.

Sulloway, F. J. (1987). "Reassessing Freud's Case Histories," *Isis*, 82: 245–275.

——— (1990). "As a Therapist, Freud Fell Short, Scholars Find," *New York Times*, March, p. C1.

INDEX